MICROCOMPUTER KEYBOARDING

SECOND EDITION

JO ANN E. SHERRON, ED.D.
J. Sargeant Reynolds Community College

RONALD H. SHERRON, PH.D.
Virginia Commonwealth University

PARADIGM

Editors Sonja Brown and Eileen Slater
Consulting Editor Dennis Gladhill
Text Designer Joan Silver
Cover Designer Pam Belding
Desktop Production Kathleen Oftedahl

ISBN 1-56118-600-7

Text + 3.5" Disk: ISBN 1-56118-602-3
Order Number: 05142

Text + 5.25" Disk: ISBN 1-56118-601-5
Order Number: 10142

Published by EMC Paradigm
875 Montreal Way
St. Paul, MN 55102
(800) 535-6865
E-mail PUBLISH@EMCP.COM

800-535-6865

Printed in the United States of America

6 7 8 9 10 XXX 99 98 97

PRINTED WITH SOY INK

15% post consumer waste

Contents

Introduction

Need for Keyboarding Skills

The rapid growth of technology, the data explosion, and the expanded use of computers in the workplace, schools, and home have increased greatly the need for keyboarding skills. Everyone is directly or indirectly influenced by computers. The person who can keyboard effectively will have an advantage both occupationally and personally in adjusting to the age of computers.

Program Purpose

This program teaches keyboarding through computer-assisted instruction. The instruction is provided by a microcomputer software program, that controls your interaction between the computer and the text. It is a self-paced program.

Learner Outcomes

After completing this program, you will be able to:

1. Use the complete microcomputer system keyboard, monitor, disks, disk drives, and printer.
2. Demonstrate proper keyboarding techniques.
3. Key straight-copy alphabetic material for three minutes at a minimum of 25 words a minute (wam) with fewer than four errors.
4. Key copy with top-row numbers using proper touch techniques at a minimum of 20 wam.
5. Key copy containing frequently used symbols at a minimum of 20 wam.
6. Key numeric copy using correct touch techniques on the ten-key numeric keypad.
7. Use selected microcomputer special function keys.
8. Develop keyboarding composition skills.
9. Understand computer terminology.

Program Design and Features

This software can be used with an IBM Personal Computer or IBM compatible. The program teaches keyboarding through individualized computer-assisted instruction using a textbook, learner disk, instructor's guide, and teacher management disk. Optional enrichment lessons offer an introduction to formatting letters, reports, and tables.

Coordinated Software and Textbook

The computer-assisted instruction of this program is coordinated with textbook instruction to provide an interactive, self-paced environment. Learners receive instruction on the screen; their input is met with either prompts, reinforcement, drill-and-practice, or word-processing screens. Speed drills also are a feature of the program. In addition to prompts and reinforcements, learners receive feedback on their performances in the form of computed speed rates and errors. The learner may enter or exit the program at will.

Computerized Recordkeeping and Grade Calculation

The Teacher Management disk is designed to assist in student recordkeeping and grade calculation. It allows teachers to assign speed and error limits. Other grading factors also can be entered—the teacher can decide what constitutes an "A" grade, a "B" grade, and so on for each exercise as well as how the different scores will be weighted in calculating final grades. Student progress can be monitored through "Measure Progress" scores, which are automatically registered on the learner record.

The Instructor's Guide gives complete information on how to operate the program and use the Teacher Management disk. It also provides suggestions for course organization, instructional procedures, and evaluation.

Research Based

This program is based on a comprehensive review of the research related to keyboarding skill acquisition and computer-assisted instruction. New concepts incorporated into this program have been field-tested with learners from a variety of backgrounds and are based on a dissertation completed by the senior author.

Individualized

This self-paced program allows the learner to move forward or backward within the lessons and to enter and exit the program when desired. The program is personalized with prompts and individual records. Minimum goals are set for each lesson. However, learners are encouraged to set higher goals for themselves as appropriate.

Flexible

This program is designed for use with the IBM Personal Computer and compatible equipment. The techniques, skills, and knowledge acquired in this program are transferable to all standard keyboards. The program can be used individually or with groups in a variety of instructional settings, such as:

1. Microcomputer keyboarding/typewriting courses.
2. Microcomputer laboratories.
3. Business and industry training.
4. Self-instruction.
5. Computer literacy courses.
6. Data entry courses.

Interdisciplinary

By using related terminology and vocabulary, the program complements other content areas such as data processing, business management, computer literacy, word processing, composition, and computer science.

Emphasis on Techniques

Correct techniques are stressed throughout the program, both in the textbook and on the microcomputer screen. Prompts and technique checks are repeated periodically along with "Get Ready" checklists.

Skill Building

In the keyboarding module, skill is increased and reinforced in each lesson through review of previously learned keys, presentation and practice of new keys, and straight-copy skill building drills. In "Measure Progress" sections, minimum performance goals are established for each lesson. These performance goals are gradually increased as the learner progresses through the program until a minimum goal of 25 wam is reached.

Performance Based

This program is goal-oriented. The program sets minimum performance goals on straight-copy material throughout the lessons. Learners have the option of increasing the goals and are encouraged to exceed these minimums. Learners progressing sequentially through the program will attain the minimum goal of 25 wam for three minutes on straight-copy material. At the end of each activity, learners are informed of their progress.

Computer-Assisted Instruction

The program uses the computer to perform a variety of instructional functions, such as:

1. Analyzing speed and indicating errors.
2. Recycling based on performance.
3. Providing prompts, reinforcements, and drill and practice.
4. Personalizing performance for each learner.
5. Maintaining learner records.
6. Providing a copy of lesson output for the learner and the teacher.

Learning Principles

This program incorporates the following research-proven learning principles.

Goal Setting

Learning is enhanced by clearly stating each lesson's objective. Minimum performance goals are given for each lesson. The learner has an option of increasing the goal for each lesson.

Drill and Practice

Each new skill and understanding is repeated and practiced until the learner reaches a selected performance level.

Immediate Feedback

Learners get immediate feedback during lessons and assessment activities. When learning new keys, misstrokes are immediately identified so the learner can key the correct response. This prevents the learner from repeating a wrong response that must later be unlearned, which can interfere with new learning.

Reinforced Learning

Reinforcement is provided in the speed drills and "Measure Progress" sections. Immediate knowledge of results is provided in the drills.

Small Increments and Spaced Practice

The program presents new material in small increments and allows for spaced practice and review of new skills and understandings. At no time is the learner overloaded with new concepts and psychomotor skill demands. This allows learners to proceed at their own pace and to experience success.

Work-related Vocabulary

The program uses examples related to the real work worlds. A fringe benefit of the program is the attainment of a basic computer literacy.

MICROCOMPUTER SYSTEM

Study the photograph to familiarize yourself with the components of a computer.

IBM Personal System 2, Model 30

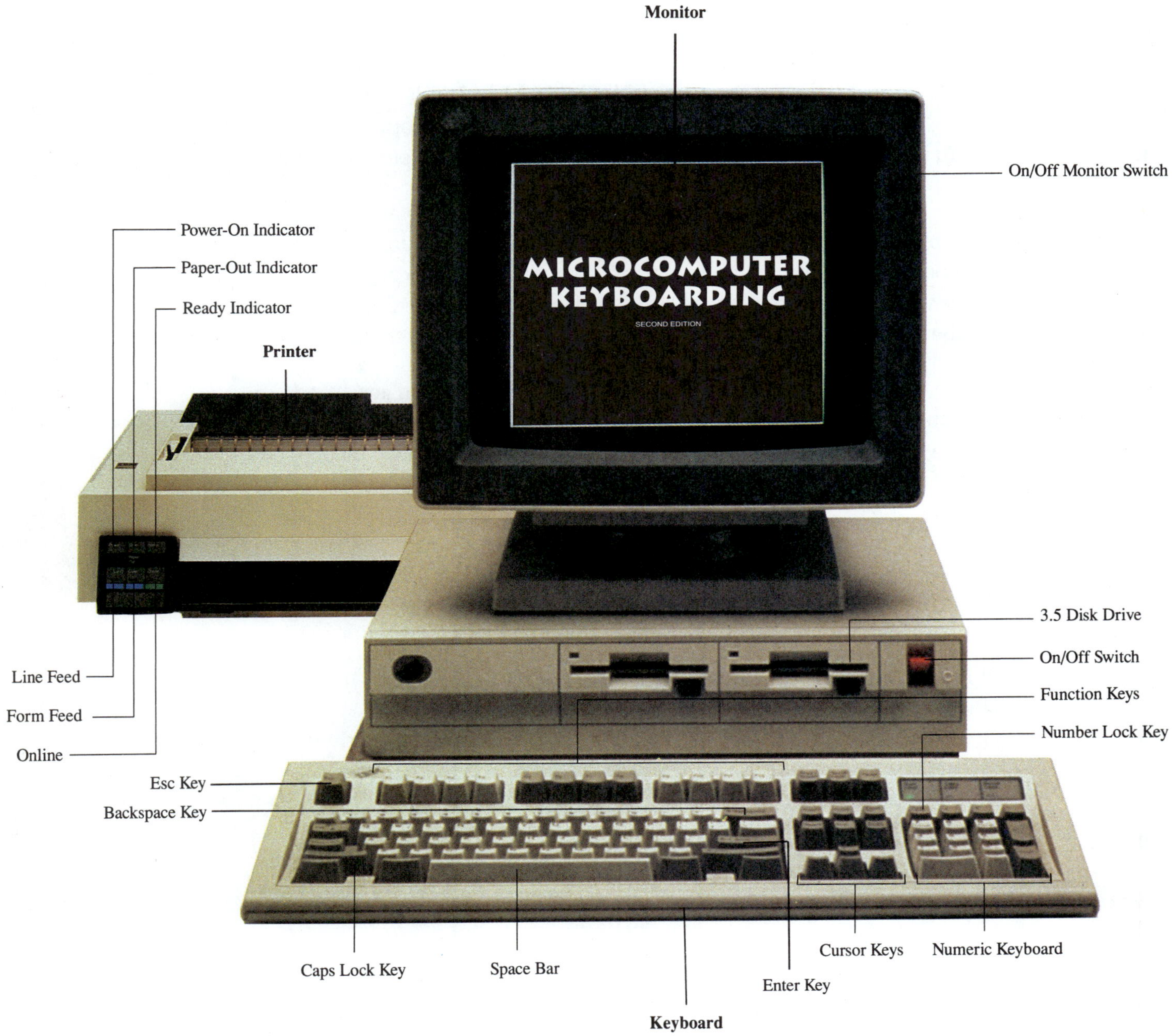

Microcomputer Operation

In order for a microcomputer to operate, whether to create original programs or to run various application programs, it must have an operating system. This Disk Operating System (DOS) is usually provided when the computer is purchased. Two common operating systems are MS-DOS and PC-DOS.

DOS tells the computer how to run software. When you "boot" your system, you are loading the DOS program. This enables the system to run any software program compatible with the DOS system. The DOS program also tells the computer how to respond to certain DOS commands entered by the user.

Once DOS is loaded onto the computer, a prompt appears on the screen. If the computer has a hard drive, a C> prompt appears. Dual or single "floppy" disk drives usually display an A> prompt. Either of these prompts indicates that the system is ready to run software programs and that the keyboard is ready to accept input.

The alphabetic and numeric keys on the microcomputer keyboard work just like a typewriter. Certain keys, however, perform functions that are unique to the software program in use. Some function keys are introduced and used in this program.

Software

The computer system will not operate without software. Software must be loaded and available to the computer system in order to perform special functions or to run a particular program.

Protect.

The software for a microcomputer system is contained on a magnetic disk—either a $3\frac{1}{2}$-inch or a $5\frac{1}{4}$-inch size. Disks are sealed in a protective cover and then inserted in a removable cover. They should be held by the corner when removing them from the outer cover. When inserting a disk into a disk drive, care should be taken not to use force. The disk should be inserted slowly and gently.

Do not bend or fold.

Insert carefully.

Never touch.

50°-125°

Never place near magnetic fields.

When handling floppy disks, there are certain precautions you must take in order not to damage them:

1. Do not fold or bend a disk.
2. Do not touch the exposed surface of the disk.
3. Do not expose a disk to extreme temperature or moisture.
4. Do not insert or remove a disk when the "in use" light or a disk drive is on.
5. After use, always store a floppy disk in its protective cover in a vertical position in a disk holder or file.
6. Do not store a disk near any magnetic or electrical fields such as monitors, telephones, or magnets.
7. Do not write on the protective cover of a $5\frac{1}{4}$-inch floppy disk with a pencil or a ballpoint pen. Write on the label provided and then attach it to the disk, or use a felt-tip pen.

Computer Keyboard

Two standard IBM keyboards are widely used in business: the enhanced keyboard and the alternate keyboard. Look at the following illustration of the enhanced keyboard. If your keyboard is arranged somewhat differently, it does not matter. The function of the keys remains the same no matter where they are located. Throughout this textbook, the "enhanced" keyboard is used for illustrations.

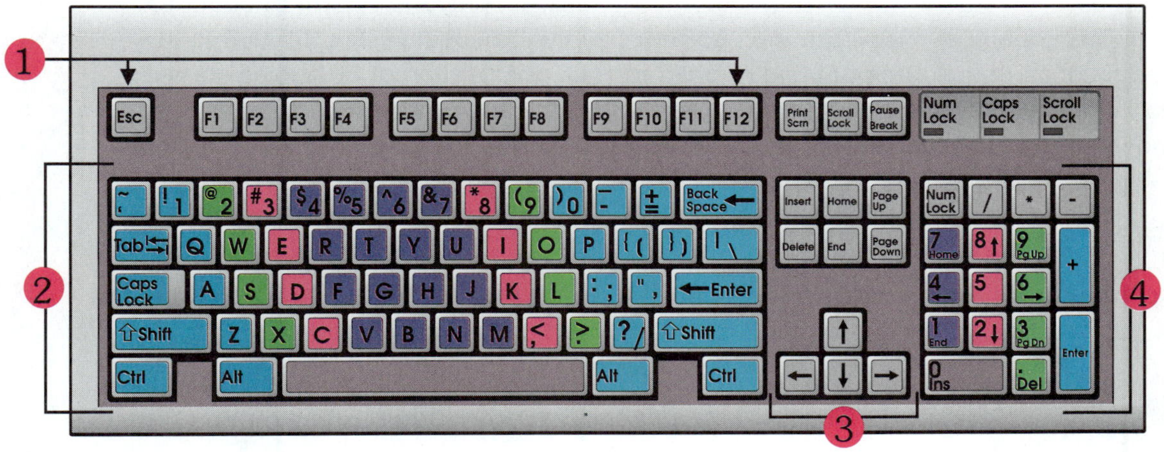

The "enhanced" microcomputer keyboard consists of four groupings of keys:

1. The function keys
2. The typewriter keys (alphabetic/numeric keyboard)
3. Cursor movement or editing keys
4. The ten-key numeric keypad

Most of the keys on either keyboard are typematic. That is, they continue to repeat their function as long as you hold them down. However, many function and editing keys act as toggle keys: pressing once turns them on, and pressing them again turns them off.

Getting Started

Equipment Required

You will need the following equipment in order to run the program provided with this textbook:

1. An IBM PC, XT, AT, PS/2 or compatible computer
2. PC-DOS or MS-DOS version 2.0 or higher
3. A monitor set for 80-column mode
4. A student program disk
5. A student data disk (blank disk for your files)
6. Access to a printer

Starting the Software

To run the software program that accompanies this textbook, you must initialize the program for your personal use. Determine which of the following systems is similar to the one you are using and then read the instructions.

Dual-Disk Computers

1. Insert the DOS disk in disk drive A.
2. Turn on the monitor and the computer.
3. When the date prompt appears, press Enter.
4. When the time prompt appears, press Enter.
5. The A> prompt should appear. (If it does not, consult your instructor.)
6. Once you have the DOS system installed on your computer, insert the student program disk in drive A and a blank formatted disk to use as a student data disk in drive B. Now key **A:** and press Enter.
7. At the A: prompt, key **MK**. A title screen will appear; press any key to continue. The first time you run the program, you will be asked to enter your full name and your I.D. number. Your instructor will assign you an I.D. The computer will mark your disk as belonging to you, so you will not need to fill in the information each time. All of your timings and scores will be saved on your data disk. In the future, continue to insert your student data disk in drive B.

Hard-Disk Computers

1. Turn on the monitor and the computer.
2. When the date prompt appears, press Enter.
3. When the time prompt appears, press Enter.
4. The C> prompt should appear.
5. At the C> prompt, key **cd** and the name of the directory in which the student program is installed. For example, you might key **cd micro**. Insert a formatted data disk into disk drive A.
6. When the name of the prompt switches to the keyboard directory, such as C:\MICRO, key **MK**. A title screen will appear; press any key to continue. The first time you run the program, you will be asked to enter your full name and your I.D. number. Your instructor will assign you an I.D. The computer will mark your disk as belonging to you, so you will not need to fill in the information each time. All of your timings and scores will be saved on your data disk. In the future, continue to insert your student data disk in drive A.

Network System

Consult your instructor to run this program on a network system.

After Initial Booting

Once the program disk is personalized for your use, you will not have to enter your name and I.D. number again. Simply insert your data disk at the appropriate prompt and key **MK**. When the title screen appears, press any key to continue. A screen similar to the following should appear. Check the information to be certain that you have the correct disk. If you have someone else's disk by mistake, press ESC to exit. Then locate your disk before you continue. If all of the information is correct, press Enter to continue.

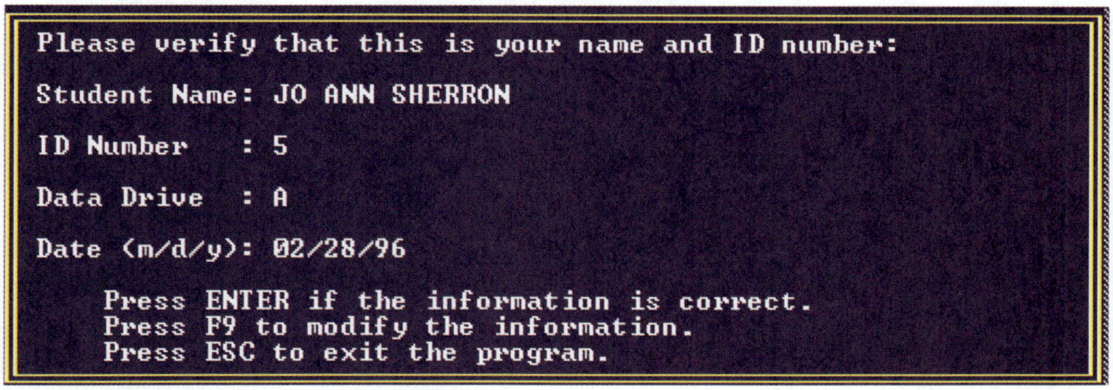

Main Menu

The *Microcomputer Keyboarding* program is organized around a series of simple "menus" that let you select what part of the program you want.

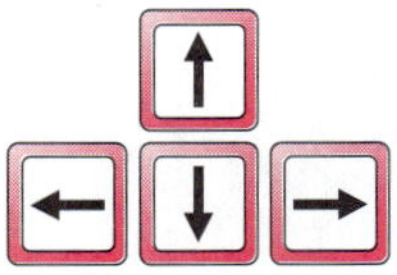

The Main Menu lists five choices, one of which is always highlighted. If you wish to begin with the highlighted choice, press Enter. To select a different choice, use the Up- and Down-Arrow keys to move the highlight. When the choice you want is highlighted, press Enter.

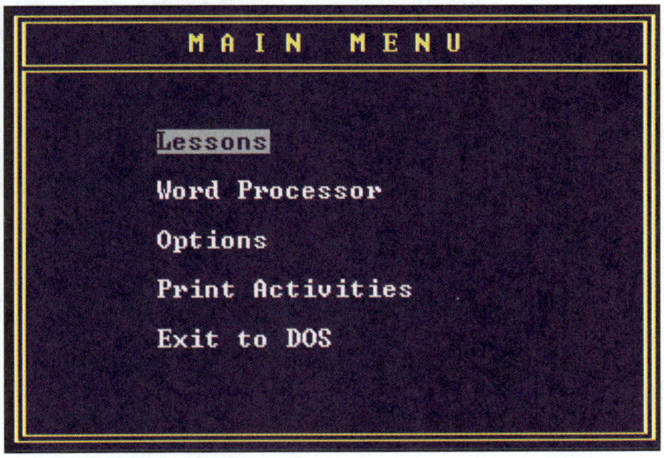

On your screen, the Main Menu looks similar to the previous illustration. Only one choice can be highlighted at a time. Selecting one of the choices will take you to one of the possible activities. A description of each activity appears below.

Lessons

This selection allows you to work with specific lessons. It is the option you will select most often. When selected, the following Lessons Menu appears.

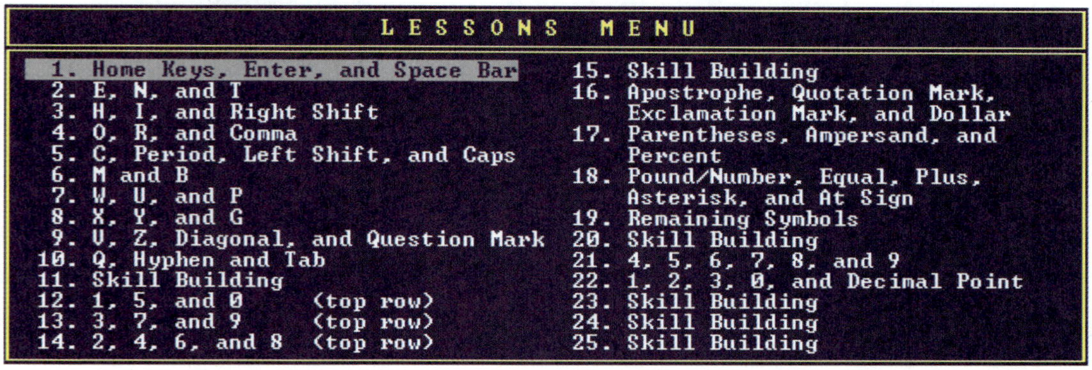

Again, one option is highlighted. Use the Up-, Down-, Left-, or Right-Arrow keys to select a specific lesson. When your choice is highlighted, press Enter. The program will take you to that lesson. Once there, follow the directions for that lesson.

Word Processor

Some of the lessons in *Microcomputer Keyboarding* contain composition and document production exercises (required or optional). In addition, your instructor may assign some special activities or timings that are not included in the textbook. These exercises are usually completed in the Word Processor option.

When Word Processor is selected, the following menu appears on the screen.

All word-processing exercises already completed appear within the box. If you wish to return to one of those documents, use the Up- and Down-Arrow keys to highlight your choice and press Enter. If you wish to create a new document, press Enter, then key the file name for the new document.

When using the Word Processor, you will be able to use the editing keys to make corrections to existing or newly created documents. Material keyed using this option can be scored for speed only. Errors will not be highlighted on the screen. Production work keyed directly from the text lessons will be graded by the computer.

Options

When a computer is booted, the software program loads default (preset) instructions for running the program. These selected settings within the program can be controlled on the options menu. When this choice is selected from the Main Menu, you can set the printer option to be compatible with the one you are using.

If the listed settings are appropriate for your hardware and for the lesson activities that you plan to complete, press ESC to return to the Main Menu. If changes are needed, press the appropriate function key listed at the bottom of the screen to change a setting. For example, if you change from a dot matrix printer to a laser printer, select F8.

Print Activities

When you select Print Activities from the Main Menu, the following screen appears.

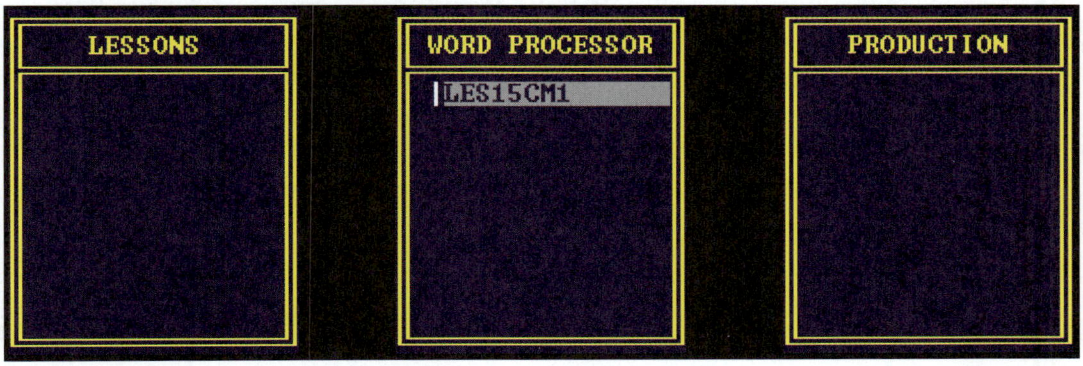

Three boxes list the document names of the last ten activities that you completed in three categories. Use the Up-, Down-, Left- and Right-Arrow keys to move the highlight to the name of the document you want to print and press Enter. If you select from the Lessons box, you will have the option to print the entire lesson or only the "Measure Progress" exercise.

If you do not have a printer connected to your computer, you can still obtain printouts of your work. When at the Main Menu, exit from the program. Remove your disk and take it to a computer connected to a printer. Boot and run your disk in the normal way. Then select Print Activities from the Main Menu. After printing, be certain to bring your disk back to your computer.

Print size is determined by the pitch setting of the printer. Pitch refers to the number of characters or spaces printed per inch. The most common pitch sizes are 10 (10 characters per inch), 12 (12 characters per inch), and 15 (15 characters per inch.) The higher the number, the smaller the print. *Microcomputer Keyboarding* defaults to 10 pitch. All exercises and word-processing documents are in 10 pitch.

Exit

The Exit option in the Main Menu allows you to leave or stop running the program at any time. If you desire to quit the program during a lesson, press ESC until the Main Menu appears and select the Exit option. When prompted, verify your intent by selecting "Yes."

Special Function Keys

Refer to page 7 for position of the function keys.

Depending on the keyboard you are using, a series of function keys is located either in a single row across the top of the keyboard or in two columns to the left of the alphabetic keyboard. Except for the ESC key, these keys have an F and a number printed on them (F1- F12 on some keyboards; F1- F10 on others). These keys "inform" the software to perform special functions according to the programmed instructions. In the *Microcomputer Keyboarding* software, certain function keys perform special actions within specific portions of the program. Some are used only while working with drills and exercises within a lesson, and others are used only when completing activities using the word processor.

The prompt line at the bottom of each screen informs you which keys are available for use at any time. If the key is not "active" and you press it, nothing will happen.

Functions keys used in *Microcomputer Keyboarding* include:

ESC Automatically takes you back to the last menu from which you made a selection. For example, if you are working in a lesson, ESC would take you back to the Lessons Contents Menu. Each time you press ESC, you will go back one more menu until you arrive at the Main Menu.

F1 Allows you to go back to the immediately preceding activity or to repeat the present activity. An "activity" is one part of a lesson such as "Review," "Increase Keying Speed," or "Improve Keying Accuracy." If you press this function key before starting an activity, you will return to the beginning of the previous activity. If you press this function key anytime after starting a particular activity, you will return to the beginning of that same activity.

F2 Allows you to skip ahead to the next activity in the lesson. If for some reason you do not wish to complete the activity presently on the screen, press this function key to move to the beginning of the next activity in the lesson sequence.

F5 Toggles between single- and double-spacing when you are in the word processor. If you press F5 to turn on the double-space format, it must be pressed again to return to single-spacing. Single-space is the default setting.

F6 Permits you to automatically center text. This is a toggle key. It centers text until you turn off the automatic centering.

F7 Allows you to change margins and set or remove tab stops while formatting in the word processor.

F10 Allows you to skip lines within a particular type of activity. A "line" is an individual item within a drill or exercise. This option cannot be used in "Measure Progress" or word-processor activities.

Each of the special function keys used in the word processor is explained and practiced when they are introduced in the textbook.

Prepare for Lesson 1

If you have not loaded the *Microcomputer Keyboarding* disk, please do it now and proceed to Lesson 1. Follow the directions on the screen to complete the lesson.

Organize Your Work Environment

A well-organized and comfortable work environment is essential to efficient keyboarding. Your work station should be uncluttered and contain only those items essential for working on the lesson. As you start each lesson, check the following:

1. Position the keyboard so it is even with the desk's front edge and slightly off-center to the left of your body.
2. If your work station is adjustable, center the monitor screen at eye level.
3. Place your book (when used) at the side of the keyboard and elevate it so that it can be clearly read.
4. If possible, adjust the monitor screen position to eliminate glare. Adjust the contrast and brightness controls for ease of viewing.

Assume Proper Posture and Correct Finger Position

Proper posture and correct finger position help prevent keying errors and fatigue. At the beginning of each lesson, do the following:

1. Place your feet flat on the floor with one foot slightly in front of the other.
2. Sit up straight with your back supported by the chair.
3. Sit the correct distance from the keyboard: drop your arms straight down by your sides and then place your fingers on the keys. If you are in the correct position, your elbows will be straight down by your sides.
4. Place your fingers on the keys in a curved position.
5. Slant your forearms at the same angle as the keyboard.
6. Keep your wrists low, but do not rest them on the keyboard.

UNIT 1-
ALPHABETIC KEYBOARD

1

Home Keys, Enter, and Space Bar

GOALS

- Learn Home Keys, Enter, and Space Bar

Get Ready

Check the following:

1. Place your feet flat on the floor with one foot slightly in front of the other.
2. Sit up straight with your back supported by the chair.
3. Sit the correct distance from the keyboard: drop your arms straight down by your sides and then place your fingers on the keys. If you are in the correct position, your elbows will be straight down by your sides.
4. Place your fingers on the home keys in a curved position.
5. Slant your forearms at the same angle as the keyboard.
6. Keep your wrists low, but do not rest them on the keyboard.

LOCATE THE HOME KEYS

Locate the home keys (A S D F J K L ;) and place your fingers on them lightly as follows.

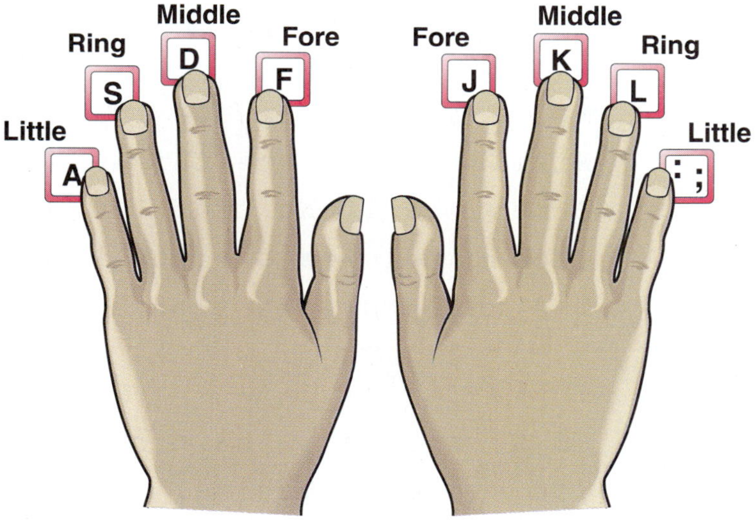

Assume proper body, hand, and finger position

Left hand:

- Little finger on the A key
- Ring finger on the S key
- Middle finger on the D key
- Forefinger on the F key

Right hand:

- Forefinger on the J key
- Middle finger on the K key
- Ring finger on the L key
- Little finger on the ; key

Practice striking the keys several times with your fingers in the proper position. Look at the screen while you key the following line.

```
asdfjkl;asdfjkl;asdfjkl;
```

Locate the Enter Key

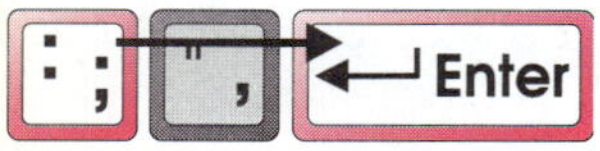

When you reach the end of a line, the Enter key is used to return the cursor to the beginning of a new line. Strike the Enter key with the little finger of your right hand.

1. Locate the Enter key.
2. With your fingers in the home key position, strike the Enter key with the little finger of your right hand (the ; finger).
3. Keep your other fingers over the home keys so that you don't lose your place.
4. Tap the Enter key quickly. Immediately return your finger to the semicolon key.

While watching the screen, practice this reach several times (; then Enter and return your finger to ;).

1 ;(Enter)

2 ;(Enter)

3 ;(Enter)

Key the following lines so that each one begins on a new line. Tap the Enter key quickly at the end of each line.

1 asdfjkl;(Enter)

2 asdfjkl;(Enter)

3 asdfjkl;(Enter)

Strike the keys quickly as if the keys were hot.

Locate the Space Bar

To leave spaces between letters or words, use the Space Bar.

1. Strike the Space Bar with your right thumb. If you are left handed, you may find it easier to use your left thumb.
2. Strike the Space Bar with a down and in motion of your thumb.
3. Look at the screen and practice keying the following:

```
asdf (space) jkl; (space) asdf (space) jkl; (space)
```

Practice the Home Keys, Enter, and Space Bar

Practice the following lines. All drill lines in all lessons should be keyed at least two times. Where indicated, use the Space Bar. At the end of a line, a ↵ appears on the screen. When you get to this symbol, strike the Enter key.

You will learn the location of the keys faster if you say each key as you strike it.

```
1 aaa ;;; sss lll ddd kkk fff jjj asdfjkl; asdfjkl;a ↵
2 ff jj dd kk ss ll aa ;; fj dk sl as las; asdf jkl; ↵
3 fj dk sl a; a ad sad fad lad fad asd as ask fad as ↵
4 all fall dad jal jad jas jaf lass flak falls flask ↵
5 jak sad fad dad jal lad fad add ask fall lass flak ↵
```

Develop Keying Skills

Do not space before a semicolon; space once after it.

Key each line two times.

```
1 adds a sad salad; asks a sad lad; a sad lass adds;
2 all dads fall; a lass asks a dad; add a fad flask;
3 a sad lass falls; all salads fall; fall dads; asks
4 ask fall lads; a lass adds; a lad falls; dad falls
5 as a fad; as all ads; as a lad asks; a salsa salad
```

End-of-Lesson Procedure

At the end of each lesson, you will have the following options:

1. To restart the same lesson, press the F1 function key.
2. To return to the Lessons Menu, press ESC. This action automatically will save the completed lesson.
3. To proceed to the next, or any other lesson, highlight your choice on the menu and press Enter.
4. To return to the Main Menu, press ESC again.
5. To print the lesson, select Print Activities.
6. To exit the program:
   a. Select the Exit option and press Enter.
   b. When the DOS prompt appears on the screen, remove your data disk.
   c. Turn off the monitor. (Your instructor also may ask you to turn off the computer and printer.)

2

E, N, and T Keys

GOALS

- Reinforce Previous Learning
- Learn New Keys E, N, and T
- Use Proper Keyboarding Techniques
- Develop Keying Skills

Get Ready

Check the following:

1. Place your feet flat on the floor with one foot slightly in front of the other.
2. Sit up straight with your back supported by the chair.
3. Sit the correct distance from the keyboard: drop your arms straight down by your sides and then place your fingers on the keys. If you are in the correct position, your elbows will be straight down by your sides.
4. Place your fingers on the home keys in a curved position.
5. Slant your forearms at the same angle as the keyboard.
6. Keep your wrists low, but do not rest them on the keyboard.

Review

Key each line two times.

Keep your fingers curved and upright.

```
1 asdfjkl; aa ;; ss ll dd kk ff jj fdsa ;lkj asdfjkl
2 asks a dad; add a salad; all dads fall; ask as dad
3 ask a dad; all lads; ask a lass; all fall; dad all
```

LOCATE THE E KEY

The E is keyed with the D finger. Place your fingers on the home keys. Look at your hands and practice the reach to E.

`ded ded ded ded`

Then look away and practice.

`ded ded ded ded`

PRACTICE THE E KEY REACH

Key each line two times.

1 ded ded deed sees keels lakes seal seeds dells ded
2 ded desks lease fakes jaded seal see leak ease fee
3 dead deaf added fled leeks sales leaf fees del ded
4 a fake; desk sales; a jaded elf asked; a deeded ad
5 see a lake; fake a seal; see a leak; eases a lease

Say each key as you strike it. Remember: Right little finger strikes Enter.

Locate the N Key

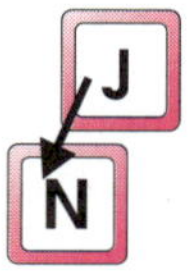

The N is keyed with the J finger. Place your fingers on the home keys. Look at your hands and practice the reach to N.

```
jnj jnj jnj jnj
```

Then look away and practice.

```
jnj jnj jnj jnj
```

Practice the N Key Reach

Key each line two times.

```
1 jnj jnj fan and land sand nan den jen ned end lend
2 ned dens ends an dan jan allen fallen fan land jan
3 nell nan and sands; dean dan; land fan; an nan and
4 fallen fan; lands and sand; land end; fall and fan
5 need all ends; and a den; and a deed; end all fads
```

Fingers are curved and upright.

LOCATE THE T KEY

Do not rest your wrists on the keyboard.

The T is keyed with the F finger. Place your fingers on the home keys. Look at your hands and practice the reach to T.

```
ftf ftf ftf ftf
```

Then look away and practice.

```
ftf ftf ftf ftf
```

PRACTICE THE T KEY REACH

Keep your other fingers on the home keys as you make the reach to T.

Key each line two times.

```
1 ftf ftf ta tans tall tale take teak teal left sets
2 tad tell at tat nest test let tee ten sat nets tan
3 ten ales; net sales; let test; tan teaks; as a lad
4 tells a tall tale; settle nest at left; ask at lad
5 tend all lakes; set a tee; lent a kale; end an elf
```

DEVELOP KEYING SKILLS

Say each key as you strike it.

Key each line two times.

```
1 tan lads take ten tall lasses salads; as all dads;
2 fallen sand settles; a fake desk sale; sales tale;
3 feds lend land fees; net sales; and ten sad teens;
4 fat ned sat; fallen sand lands; as last tests sat;
5 all ants eat kale; ease all lakes; sale fell flat;
```

Measure Progress

Each Measure Progress exercise in this text presents a minimum goal for words-a-minute (wam) performance. In all these timed drills, the software automatically will compute your keying speed. In computing keying speed, the software counts every five strokes (including spaces and punctuation marks) as a word. Keying speed is reported as an average of words keyed in one minute (wam).

A prompt will appear on the monitor before starting the exercise. You may either accept the stated minimum goal or set a higher speed goal. If you do not want to change the minimum goal, enter N at the prompt. If you wish to set a higher goal, enter Y at the prompt and enter the higher goal. You are encouraged to set a higher goal to challenge yourself.

Take two 1-minute timings on the following group of lines. Read the copy from the book and key the lines on the computer. The computer will calculate the speed, record the score, determine if your goal was met, and indicate the next activity. If you complete the drill before time runs out, begin again.

Minimum goal: 10 wam

Key quickly.

```
1 a fallen desk lands; tan lass falls; send as fast;
2 tan lasses talked; ten teak desks; dads lend; asks
3 daff lads sass dads; fallen tasks; takes ten; lads
  □□□□1□□□□2□□□□3□□□□4□□□□5□□□□6□□□□7□□□□8□□□□9□□□10
```

End-of-Lesson Procedure

At the end of each lesson, you will have the following options:

1. To restart the same lesson, press the F1 function key.
2. To return to the Lessons Menu, press ESC. This action automatically will save the completed lesson.
3. To proceed to the next, or any other lesson, highlight your choice on the menu and press Enter.
4. To return to the Main Menu, press ESC again.
5. To print the lesson, select Print Activities.
6. To exit the program:
   a. Select the Exit option and press Enter.
   b. When the DOS prompt appears on the screen, remove your data disk.
   c. Turn off the monitor. (Your instructor also may ask you to turn off the computer and printer.)

3

H, I, and Right Shift Keys

GOALS

- Reinforce Previous Learning
- Learn New Keys H, I, and Right Shift
- Develop Keying Skills

Get Ready

Check the following:

1. Place your feet flat on the floor with one foot slightly in front of the other.
2. Sit up straight with your back supported by the chair.
3. Sit the correct distance from the keyboard.
4. Place your fingers on the home keys in a curved position.
5. Slant your forearms at the same angle as the keyboard.
6. Keep your wrists low, but do not rest them on the keyboard.

Review

Remember to key all drill lines two times.

```
1 asdfjkl; aa ;; ss ll dd kk ff jj ded jnj ftf asdfj
2 task all dads; fallen desk lands; ask all tan lads
3 lasses ask daff lads; dad sets nets; a flask; ants
4 a fake desk sale; a jaded elf asked; all deaf lads
```

Strike each key quickly as if it were hot.

LOCATE THE H KEY

H ← J

The H is keyed with the J finger. Place your fingers on the home keys. Look at your hands and practice the reach to H.

```
jhj jhj jhj jhj
```

Then look away and practice.

```
jhj jhj jhj jhj
```

PRACTICE THE H KEY REACH

Keep your fingers curved and upright. Keep your other fingers on the home keys. Strike Enter with your little finger.

Key each line two times.

```
1 jhj jhj had halls has held she the that has dashes
2 that ahead hate had hal heal shell shed hat health
3 he shall lash that shaft at the sale; slant at ash
4 the fallen lash landed at that desk; has she asked
5 he has the shells; she has that shed; he had that;
```

Locate the I Key

The I is keyed with the K finger. Place your fingers on the home keys. Look at your hands and practice the reach to I.

```
kik kik kik kik
```

Then look away and practice.

```
kik kik kik kik
```

Practice the I Key Reach

Your J finger may lift slightly, but keep your other fingers on the home keys.

Key each line two times.

```
1 kik kik kits kite lite site lids diet slid fits ki
2 it sit sift list fit is aid said knit kit hit sits
3 kid slid; kite kits; site list; sift it; it is his
4 kids said knit; lite lit site; it said aid; hit it
5 that site did fit; she said that last tent failed;
```

Locate the Right ⇧Shift Key

Use the Shift keys to make capital letters. To capitalize left-hand letters, use the Right Shift key. When you operate the Right Shift key, use a three-step procedure:

1. Press the Right Shift key with your right little finger and hold it down. (Keep your J and K fingers on the home keys.)
2. Strike the letter you want capitalized with the correct left-hand finger.
3. Release the Shift key and return your little finger immediately to the ; key.

Look at your hands and practice the following:

Al; Al; Al; Al;

Practice the Right ⇧Shift Key Reach

Remember:
1. Depress Right Shift key.
2. Strike key with left-hand finger.
3. Release Shift key and return to home position.

Key each line two times.

1 Ada Ella Dad Eli Edna Dale Elsa Sandi Ella Fae Alf
2 Desk Dad Ten Dad lends Ella a desk; Did the sales;
3 Take ten ales; the fallen desk lands; Dad asks Ali
4 Dad did kid Ella; Tadd asks dad; Tan teak sets she
5 Ella asked Ted and Tina; The desk fell and hit Eli

Develop Keying Skills

Strike each key quickly and sharply.

Key each line two times.

1 an is if it hi fi tea sea tan fat dad had sad has;
2 net set let all tall fall hens had a desk ask dad;
3 A jaded elf asked; Ten tan lads; Takes salads; Fan
4 Dad had a fat hen; The lads had ten hits; Ask Til;
5 Tell Ed ask Tad; did sell; Talie and Elese failed;

Increase Keying Speed

Now you will have a chance to race against the computer. Key the following sentences quickly. Strike the Space Bar at the end of each word. Do not space at the end of a line; strike the Enter key quickly. Try to beat the computer. If you finish before the moving light bar gets to the end of the line, you win! Key each line twice. Try to improve your speed the second time.

Snap your finger toward your palm after each stroke. Key quickly.

```
1 As it is;
2 See if it and
3 Tea is fit as ale;
4 Tall let ask set tin
5 At all is lad feel till
```

□□□□1□□□□2□□□□3□□□□4□□□□5□□□□6□□□□7□□□□8□□□□9□□□10

Key the lines again. Try to key them in less time.

Measure Progress

Take two 1-minute timings on the following group of lines. Read the copy from the book and key the lines on the computer. The computer will calculate the speed and record your score. If you complete the drill before time runs out, begin again.

Minimum goal: 11 wam

```
1 Ten tall tan lads sent dad a teak desk; As it has;
2 Tad lends Dela a tent; if it is inside the salads;
3 A jaded elf asked a fat lad; Tell Ella Fae a tale;
```

□□□□1□□□□2□□□□3□□□□4□□□□5□□□□6□□□□7□□□□8□□□□9□□□10

End-of-Lesson Procedure

At the end of each lesson, you will have the following options:

1. To restart the same lesson, press the F1 function key.
2. To return to the Lessons Menu, press ESC. This action automatically will save the completed lesson.
3. To proceed to the next, or any other lesson, highlight your choice on the menu.
4. To return to the Main Menu, press ESC again.
5. To print the lesson, select Print Activities.
6. To exit the program:
   a. Select the Exit option and press Enter.
   b. When the DOS prompt appears on the screen, remove your data disk.
   c. Turn off the monitor. (Your instructor also may ask you to turn off the computer and printer.)

4

O, R, and Comma Keys

GOALS

- Reinforce Previous Learning
- Learn New Keys O, R, and Comma
- Develop Keying Skills

Get Ready

Check the following:

1. Place your feet flat on the floor with one foot slightly in front of the other.
2. Sit up straight with your back supported by the chair.
3. Sit the correct distance from the keyboard.
4. Place your fingers on the home keys in a curved position.
5. Slant your forearms at the same angle as the keyboard.
6. Keep your wrists low, but do not rest them on the keyboard.

Review

Key each line two times.

Space quickly. Do not pause.

1 asdf jkl; aa ;; ss ll dd kk ff jjj ded ded jnj jnj
2 ftf ftf jhj jhj kik kik tent hill heat hidden heel
3 desk sea see leak ease a fake title sale as if has
4 Tad lends Annie ten tan sandals; Takes ten stands;

Locate the O Key

The O is keyed with the L finger. Place your fingers on the home keys. Look at your hands and practice the reach to O.

```
lol lol lol lol
```

Then look away and practice.

```
lol lol lol lol
```

Practice the O Key Reach

Key each line two times.

```
1 lol lol look old told do does of so done doll fold
2 to do so of foods jot dots oaks sold loads off ton
3 does doses took nose toes foes also floss dole nod
4 not lost son ton tod off old too sod oaks odd oils
5 done told joke host loan knot look loss also stood
6 load food folks noise toast lesson stole to one of
7 Do old folks also do the salad; Sold one old food;
```

Keep your J and K fingers on the home keys. Your ; finger may lift slightly.

LOCATE THE R KEY

The R is keyed with the F finger. Place your fingers on the home keys. Look at your hands and practice the reach to R.

```
frf frf frf frf
```

Then look away and practice.

```
frf frf frf frf
```

PRACTICE THE R KEY REACH

Remember to keep your other fingers on the home keys.

Key each line two times.

```
1  frf frf forts rode rids rods or for jars risks red
2  areas first order after dears dare drain error ran
3  for rot roll are ear her ran rat jar tar far floor
4  tar ark era art rid rare rain dark order tree area
5  sir fir dear rear rake rest roast store other rate
6  dare dress stare horn torn front stair there their
7  fair risk after heart shirt their tired real there
8  letter are enrolled stern reasons desert steer tar
9  These Fords took a load of tar ore; toss a rose on
10 Take the order for trees; this note is not for her
```

LOCATE THE <, KEY

Within a sentence, do not space before a comma; space once after it.

The , (comma) is keyed with the K finger. Place your fingers on the home keys. Look at your hands and practice the reach to , . Remember: Within a sentence, do not space before a comma; space once after it.

```
k,k k,k k,k k,k
```

Then look away and practice.

```
k,k k,k k,k k,k
```

PRACTICE THE <, KEY REACH

Your J finger may lift slightly, but keep your other fingers on the home keys.

Key each line two times.

```
1 k,k k,k Ron, Alf, Ann, deserts, letters, reason of
2 Stole a train ride for Eddie, Ronald, Ann, and Don
3 Send Annie roses, jade, jars, sand, tea, and tires
4 Files, letters, folders, and a list are in a desk;
5 The sandals, dress, and shoes fit Sheila and Terri
```

DEVELOP KEYING SKILLS

Say each key as you strike it. Key and space quickly—do not pause.

Key each line two times.

```
1 Take an order for ten trees, Teak desks are in it;
2 Send fees for Tad, Al, Te, and Ann, Feds sent land
3 Ask all sales lads to send net sales on rod deeds,
4 The order is for jars, teak, tests, tires, and sod
5 Slate the latest list of net sales, send the deed;
```

Measure Progress

Take two 1-minute timings on the following group of lines. Read the copy from the book and key the lines on the computer. The computer will calculate the speed and record your score. If you complete the drill before time runs out, begin again.

Minimum goal: 12 wam

Key quickly.

```
1 it is inside a load of lost ores on the old Fords;
2 Toss roses to lasses; Ask Don to lend Andi a tire;
3 Send fees for Tal, Ronald, Edna, and Sid; stole it
      1    2    3    4    5    6    7    8    9   10
```

End-of-Lesson Procedure

At the end of each lesson, you will have the following options:

1. To restart the same lesson, press the F1 function key.
2. To return to the Lessons Menu, press ESC. This action automatically will save the completed lesson.
3. To proceed to the next, or any other lesson, highlight your choice on the menu and press Enter.
4. To return to the Main Menu, press ESC again.
5. To print the lesson, select Print Activities.
6. To exit the program:
   a. Select the Exit option and press Enter.
   b. When the DOS prompt appears on the screen, remove your data disk.
   c. Turn off the monitor. (Your instructor also may ask you to turn off the computer and printer.)

5

C, Period, Left Shift, and Caps Lock Keys

GOALS

- Reinforce Previous Learning
- Learn New Keys C, Period, Left Shift, and Caps Lock
- Develop Keying Skills

Get Ready checklist:

1. Feet flat.
2. Sit straight.
3. Elbows by side.
4. Fingers curved, upright.
5. Slant forearms.
6. Wrists low but not on keyboard.

REVIEW

Key each line two times.

```
1 asdfjkl; fdsa; lkj ded ded ftf ftf jnj jnj kik kik
2 jhj lol lol frf frf k,k k,k or, old sold told rode
3 A load of ore tested a tired lad; one fallen rose;
4 Ask De Ann to floss teeth often, lasses tossed it;
```

LOCATE THE C KEY

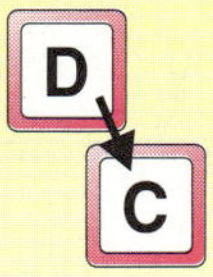

The C is keyed with the D finger. Place your fingers on the home keys. Look at your hands and practice the reach to C.

```
dcd dcd dcd dcd
```

Then look away and practice.

```
dcd dcd dcd dcd
```

PRACTICE THE C KEY REACH

Your F finger may lift slightly, but keep your other fingers on the home keys.

Key each line two times.

```
1 dcd dcd call cards credit can class office car cats
2 cakes cads casks calls decades scale cod docks cots
3 car can cell ace cake deck face cook coke case care
4 cask call cool cord coil cool cede cash cast decade
5 cane card cash calf since chase ancient chain scale
6 cease classes credit decease career corn calk notch
7 corn cook calk finance circle notice coin cook cane
8 cases jacks cease accord concern cad cost face coat
9 Cathi called the offices; the clock ticks, accessed
10 Cal can cook a cake, it is the circle in the field;
```

LOCATE THE > KEY

Space twice after a period at the end of a sentence. Space once after a period in an abbreviation.

The . (period) is keyed with the L finger. Place your fingers on the home keys. Look at your hands and practice the reach to the period key. Remember: Space twice after a period at the end of a sentence. Space once after a period in an abbreviation.

```
l.l l.l l.l l.l
```

Then look away and practice.

```
l.l l.l l.l l.l
```

PRACTICE THE > KEY REACH

Keep your fingers curved and your J and K fingers on the home keys.

Your ; finger may lift slightly.

Key each line two times.

1 l.l l.l Si is. Call Rae. Tell Candie. Ask Carl.
2 Dan Cane is in the A. R. S. in SD. Al is not ill.
3 El is late for dinner. The thief left the island.
4 Allen has landed the jet. Dennis failed the test.
5 Dona and Ted had an old clock at the sales office.
6 Dee had a class fan in the old jet dock for Salli.

LOCATE THE LEFT ⇧Shift KEY

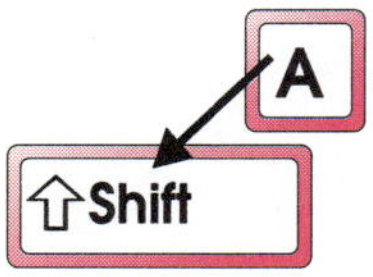

To capitalize right-hand letters, use the Left Shift key. When you operate the Left Shift key, use a three-step procedure:

1. Press the Left Shift key with your left little finger and hold it down. (Keep your F and D fingers on the home keys.)
2. Strike the letter you want capitalized with the correct right-hand finger.
3. Release the Shift key and return your finger immediately to the A key.

Look at your hands and practice the following:

Ja Ja Ja Ja

Remember:

1. **Depress the Left Shift key.**
2. **Strike the key with correct right-hand finger.**
3. **Release the Left Shift key and return to home position.**

Practice the Left Shift Key Reach

Key each line two times.

```
1 Jan Kal Hal Jack Lan Jeff Kitt Ken Joe Lea Les Kit
2 Kent and Joe see Jeff; Kal asks Les, Jo, and Lara.
3 Hank sells dads a teak desk son; Ken asked Leslie.
4 Order these:  Cartons, Jacks, Clocks, Dolls, Jars.
```

The colon in line 4 is the shift of the semicolon. Space twice after a colon used as punctuation.

Locate the Caps Lock Key

To key a series of letters or words in all capital letters, use the Caps Lock key. The Caps Lock key is located on either the left or right side of the keyboard. It is operated with the appropriate little finger. Locate the Caps Lock key on your keyboard.

Follow these steps when keying words or sentences in all caps:

1. Depress the Caps Lock key with the little finger.
2. Enter the letters to be capitalized.
3. Depress the Caps Lock key again. This releases the all caps feature. (The Caps Lock key is a toggle switch.)

When the Caps Lock key is on, only the alphabetic keys are affected. The shift key must still be used to key a colon or symbol.

PRACTICE THE Caps Lock KEY REACH

Key each line two times.

1 THE CONTRACT CASE CONCERNED THE CONDO ORDER TAKER.
2 KARL and LINDA and CHRIS and CINDA and CATHE left.
3 The TEN ANCIENT RAKES is the title that JANE read.

DEVELOP KEYING SKILLS

Key each line two times.

Your fingers should not fly around but should be poised over the keyboard.

Let your fingers do the work—not your wrists.

1 Todd sold one clock; Jan sells docks and tan sand.
2 The cat ate the rat; Ten teals left the nest neat.
3 Tell Ken, Lara, Joel, Jeff, and Hank to call Jane.
4 Then HAL and JES tossed that fish on the old dock.
5 Dear Ron: Dear Carol: Dear Ted: Dear Catherine:
6 Janet told Rosanne to notice the financial losses.
7 The folks stood to stare at the area flood fronts.
8 The cash cards are essential for a finance career.
9 An ancient cane rake is their reason to notice it.
10 The credit classes are also the other cash lesson.

MEASURE PROGRESS

Take two 1-minute timings.

Minimum goal: 13 wam

Key quickly.

1 Net sales for that first art soared for Lara Anne.
2 These Feds leased the trash lands for local areas.
3 Leslie said that local ore lands on the last dock.

□□□□1□□□□2□□□□3□□□□4□□□□5□□□□6□□□□7□□□□8□□□□9□□□10

END-OF-LESSON PROCEDURE

At the end of each lesson, you will have the following options:

1. To restart the same lesson, press the F1 function key.
2. To return to the Lessons Menu, press ESC.
3. To proceed to the next, or any other lesson, make your choice on the menu.
4. To print the lesson, select Print Activities.
5. To exit the program:
   a. Select the Exit option and press Enter.
   b. When the DOS prompt appears on the screen, remove your data disk.
   c. Turn off the monitor and/or computer.

6 Skill Building

GOALS

- Reinforce Previous Learning
- Increase Keying Speed

Get Ready checklist:

1. Feet flat.
2. Sit straight.
3. Elbows by side.
4. Fingers curved, upright.
5. Slant forearms.
6. Wrists low but not on keyboard.

REVIEW

Key each line two times.

1 all dads fall; a lass asks a dad; add a fad flask;
2 a sad lass falls; all salads fall; fall dads; asks
3 ask all lads; a lass adds; a lad falls; lass falls
4 as a fad; as all ads; as a lad asks; a salsa salad

DEVELOP KEYING SKILLS

Key each line two times.

1 ask a dad; all lads; ask a lass; all fall; dad all
2 dead deaf added fled leeks sales leaf fees del den
3 see a lease; fake a seal; see a leak; eases a sail
4 need all ends; and a den; and a deed; end all fads
5 tells a tall tale; settle nest at left; ask at lad
6 tend all lakes; set a tee; lent a kale; end an elf
7 kid slid; kite kits; site list; sift it; it is his
8 Dad did kid Ella; Tadd asks Dad; Tan teak sets she
9 the fallen lash landed at that desk; has she asked
10 kids said knit; lite lit site; it said aid; hit it
11 Tad lends Annie ten tan sandals; Takes ten stands;

Increase Keying Speed

Key each line two times. Try to increase your speed on the second time.

Race to beat the computer.

1 Ted sets a date; all fish seek the seas and lakes;
2 look one thin foal sold; that fool told old jokes;
3 Ronn rakes rare red roses after the rain and hail;
4 Those letters on disk and data files are not rare;
5 dent a tent; last fat ant; tell tall tales to Ted,
6 Ella asked Ted and Tina; The desk fell and hit Eli
7 Desk Dad Ten Dad lends Ella a desk; Did the sales;
8 fallen fan; lands and sand; land end; fall and fan
9 all ants eat kale; ease all lakes; sale fell flat;
10 that ahead hate had has heal shell shed hat health
11 A faded elf asked; Ten tan lads; Takes salads; Fan
12 he shall lash that trash at the sale; slant at ash
□□□□1□□□□2□□□□3□□□□4□□□□5□□□□6□□□□7□□□□8□□□□9□□□10

Measure Progress

Take two 1-minute timings.

Minimum goal: 13 wam

1 fallen sand settles; a fake desk sale; sales tale;
2 that site did fit; she said that last tent failed;
3 Dad had a fat hen; The lads had ten hits; Ask Til;
□□□□1□□□□2□□□□3□□□□4□□□□5□□□□6□□□□7□□□□8□□□□9□□□10

End-of-Lesson Procedure

At the end of each lesson, you will have the following options:

1. To restart the same lesson, press the F1 function key.
2. To return to the Lessons Menu, press ESC.
3. To proceed to the next, or any other lesson, make your choice on the menu.
4. To return to the Main Menu, press ESC again.
5. To print the lesson, select Print Activities.
6. To exit the program:
   a. Select the Exit option and press Enter.
   b. When the DOS prompt appears on the screen, remove your data disk.
   c. Turn off the monitor. (Your instructor also may ask you to turn off the computer and printer.)

7

M and B Keys

GOALS

- Reinforce Previous Learning
- Learn New Keys M and B
- Develop Keying Skills
- Increase Keying Speed

Review the "Get Ready" checklist.

Review

Key each line two times.

1 `jnj jnj ftf ftf jhj jhj kik kik lol lol dcd dcd fr`

2 `cakes casks calf coat coach cocoa cocoon coed coin`

3 `The ashes of the trash landed on that one old dock`

4 `Ask Al, Kit, Jan, and Tod to access the CAD class.`

5 `NAL leases land to:  Jeff, Ona, Ci, Carl, and Cil.`

Locate the M Key

The M is keyed with the J finger. Place your fingers on the home keys. Look at your hands and practice the reach to M.

`jmj jmj jmj jmj`

Then look away and practice.

jmj jmj jmj jmj

Practice the M Key Reach

Key each line two times.

1 jmj jmj me mat met ham him tam make same fame home
2 dim aim mat same milk then them miss remit dreamed
3 elm jam Kim man mad dim time farm male metal admit
4 rim Mrs. Ms. farm main came cane them smile almost
5 arm mad mint seem harm make maid melts accommodate
6 mail come memo team ream seam mats meet mode small
7 Small teams made the main model memo come to fame.
8 Ask Matt to send me those metal milk cartons soon.
9 Fame comes to most men: Men met at the same time.
10 Admit as many teams as the memorial home may mass.

Keep your fingers curved and on the home keys.

Locate the B Key

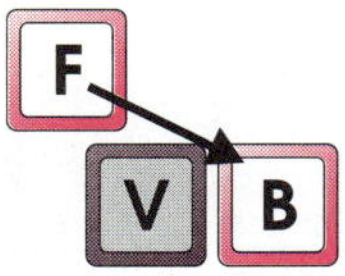

The B is keyed with the F finger. Place your fingers on the home keys. Look at your hands and practice the reach to B.

fbf fbf fbf fbf

Then look away and practice.

fbf fbf fbf fbf

PRACTICE THE B KEY REACH

Key each line two times.

Use proper technique.

1 fbf fbf fibs lib rib bit be bat base ball baseball
2 bar herb debit ballet bet bald credit fiber border
3 bit bite ballot booklet black amber labor dab bell
4 Bob barb label bread remember blast job bear blast
5 Ben bare object alibi better mob belt harbor block
6 mob bee dab book back beef best debt bend bias ban
7 rob file better fiber object able debt booklet bar
8 bad beds black books blocks belts booklet boat bit
9 Cobie asked the Feds to bid on the old bank books.
10 Notice a bank bid; a bank booklet boasts all jobs.

DEVELOP KEYING SKILLS

Key each line two times.

As you repeat each line, try to key it faster.

1 ded jnj ftf jhj kik lol frf dcd jmj fbf l.l k,k ;;
2 he be in on so do or it am if do ha ma to ti is as
3 an and for the hot ten lie dim din too bid did rid
4 coin cake came jack half roll mine site bake hates
5 he is in,so it is,if he is,or he is or,be at,be me
6 can she see,and for him,she had all,did not,bit it
7 Arnie; Fred; Jamie; Sam; Samantha; Dennis; Denise;
8 I can do it if I see all the hats in the old mall.
9 So the bold cats ran for the rat on that cold mat.
10 Order these for Randi: coins, markers, and beads.

Increase Keying Speed

Key each line two times.

Try to beat the computer and improve your speed on the second try. Check your speed as noted by the computer.

1 Most men limit times for comments. Bob made bits.
2 The last absences of both bosses are not abnormal.
3 The ten sales told the bankers to net that credit.
4 Madams and men make more comments than the lasses.
5 The time for sane comments is not before the meet.
6 Lease the land that has this oar. Take the books.
7 Both boats blocked the load of ore. Take her car.
8 The absence of the boss from her job left him mad.
9 Remember to accommodate the bank credit and debit.
10 The ballet dancer dreamed of a model dance career.
11 Admit a blast from the harbor jolted the main rim.
12 She is. It is. Ask Mark. Tell Bill. Call Bart.
13 Lt. Marke is a member of the A. M. B. in the A. F.

□□□□1□□□□2□□□□3□□□□4□□□□5□□□□6□□□□7□□□□8□□□□9□□□10

Measure Progress

Take two 1-minute timings.

Minimum goal: 14 wam

Key quickly.

1 Small fees make most banks mad. Send books to me.
2 The land leases left those men mad and then broke.
3 Lads send lasses red roses. That clock ticks Ben.

□□□□1□□□□2□□□□3□□□□4□□□□5□□□□6□□□□7□□□□8□□□□9□□□10

End-of-Lesson Procedure

1. To restart the same lesson, press the F1 function key.
2. To return to the Lessons Menu, press ESC.
3. To proceed to another lesson, make your choice on the menu.
4. To return to the Main Menu, press ESC again.
5. To print the lesson, select Print Activities.
6. To exit the program:
   a. Select the Exit option and press Enter.
   b. When the DOS prompt appears on the screen, remove your data disk.
   c. Turn off the monitor. (Your instructor may ask you to turn off the computer and printer.)

8

W, U, and P Keys

GOALS

- Reinforce Previous Learning
- Learn New Keys W, U, and P
- Increase Keying Speed

Remember the "Get Ready" checklist.

Review

Key each line two times.

```
1 jkj kik lol frf dcd jmj jmj k,k fbf fbf l.l books.
2 Ask Al, Ted, and Ken to test the first sales kits.
3 The credit card net sales concern all small banks.
4 The bids for that leased land had a bank late fee.
5 Most men belt BASEBALLS.  Three bids came in late.
```

Locate the W Key

The W is keyed with the S finger. Place your fingers on the home keys and practice the reach to W.

```
sws sws sws sws
```

Practice the W Key Reach

Key each line two times.

1 sws sws saw was cows how now we will with saw wads
2 who jaw well draw snow town down water elbow where
3 new now won workable know word flow wisdom awkward
4 web few west swim waken shown woman awkward follow
5 raw two walk swell window write hardware twin draw
6 weakness saw win law welfare warmer between follow
7 Will worked with Wat. Win wanted it to snow fast.
8 Walker wished we knew where that bank was located.
9 William wanted that snow to land on the west bank.
10 Mrs. Woodard wants the hardware to be well worked.

Keep your other fingers in home key position.

Locate the U Key

The U is keyed with the J finger. Place your fingers on the home keys and practice the reach to U.

juj juj juj juj

Practice the U Key Reach

Key each line two times.

1 juj juj jure just juts jute due ruts tuts muts use
2 out rub bulb hunt adult usual assure insure ensure
3 sun fun duel soul just rust nurse under module cut
4 mud turn fund uses fault build rumor fusion endure
5 but auto full fuel club sure junk true fourth shut
6 must truth audit usual manual musical rubbed about
7 refund actual just fault rub cut under build nurse
8 rush us brush sue due uses fused untie usual fruit
9 Our annual runs for fun should break that account.
10 The lures were a must to catch the four blue fish.

Practice keying while keeping your eyes on the copy.

Locate the P Key

The P is keyed with the ; finger. Place your fingers on the home keys and practice the reach to P.

;p; ;p; ;p; ;p;

PRACTICE THE P KEY REACH

Key each line two times.

1 ;p; ;p; ;p; pie pies pan pans piers pens maps pats
2 tap tape part price planet staple purpose percents
3 per plain hope happen person possible stop pail up
4 past people elapse napkin present special trip lap
5 appeal please support purpose price possible slain
6 hope part prices proper police past plain prim pad
7 These projects were not presented in proper plans.
8 Put pen on paper to write about personal problems.
9 Paul put staples on the tape per specific purpose.
10 The price of the pen part was too deep to present.

Use proper technique; check fingers and wrists.

INCREASE KEYING SPEED

Try to beat the computer. Key quickly.

1 All the banks can insure new credit card accounts.
2 A desk has four deep drawers for files and others.
3 Wallace told Sam and Kim to take the old teak pot.
4 Most banks like credit cards and that account fee.
5 The proper police accounts were filed on the disk.
6 The two black boats landed ten blues on that deck.
7 Joe lets annual land leases to banks for branches.
8 Williams wished we had known when the police came.
9 The woman walked the usual laps without a purpose.
10 Ms. White supported the special fuel price refund.

□□□□1□□□□2□□□□3□□□□4□□□□5□□□□6□□□□7□□□□8□□□□9□□□10

Keep your eyes on the copy—do not watch your hands.

MEASURE PROGRESS

Take two 1-minute timings.

Minimum goal: 15 wam

Key quickly.

```
1 Net sales for that leased land told those men how.
2 This plain clock had two old warped, purple hands.
3 A man named Wilbur called to make her appointment.
  □□□□1□□□□2□□□□3□□□□4□□□□5□□□□6□□□□7□□□□8□□□□9□□□10
```

END-OF-LESSON PROCEDURE

At the end of each lesson, you will have the following options:

1. To restart the same lesson, press the F1 function key.
2. To return to the Lessons Menu, press ESC. This action automatically will save the completed lesson.
3. To proceed to the next, or any other lesson, highlight your choice on the menu and press Enter.
4. To return to the Main Menu, press ESC again.
5. To print the lesson, select Print Activities.
6. To exit the program:
   a. Select the Exit option and press Enter.
   b. When the DOS prompt appears on the screen, remove your data disk.
   c. Turn off the monitor. (Your instructor also may ask you to turn off the computer and printer.)

9 X, Y, and G Keys

GOALS

- Reinforce Previous Learning
- Learn New Keys X, Y, and G
- Increase Keying Speed

Remember the "Get Ready" checklist.

Review

Key each line two times.

1 dcd dcd jmj jmj fbf fbf l.l l.l sws sws juj juj ;p

2 Wheel winner whether weather where pamphlet panic,

3 Parallel parent participate partition umbrella use

4 The winner decided not to keep the old blue pumps.

5 Warren and Carroll entered the annual run for fun.

Locate the X Key

The X is keyed with the S finger. Place your fingers on the home keys and practice the reach to X.

sxs sxs sxs sxs

Practice the X Key Reach

Key each line two times.

1 sxs sxs six fox fix axe ox six flex ax relax foxes
2 tax taxes next boxes complex exams Tex oxen ox wax
3 box next axle exhaust annex except excellent index
4 six excel text sixth export exact expedite mixture
5 extra extend express anxious maximum excellent box
6 expect exist deluxe excess excellent fix exact six
7 examine excels expedite approximate next axle text
8 Excellent expense report is as usual lax in taxes.
9 Six oxen flexed for Texas. Completed exams taxed.
10 Maxie examined the express text to expedite exams.
11 The approximate cost of the maximum expenses fell.

As you key the X, your A finger may lift slightly. Keep your other fingers in home key position.

Locate the Y Key

The Y is keyed with the J finger. Place your fingers on the home keys and practice the reach to Y.

jyj jyj jyj jyj

PRACTICE THE Y KEY REACH

Key each line two times.

Key quickly and use proper technique.

```
1  jyj jyj yarn yet say plays lays pays types yet hay
2  pay copy type company money yellow yachts spy yawn
3  may obey yearly okay fully daily rhyme family they
4  policy system defy likely yield today study supply
5  fry easy maybe property company luxury rhyme daily
6  try styles study employees yields day easy yes may
7  All my new yearly net yields fluctuate like yoyos.
8  My yearly study of employees pay was not too easy.
9  Tony can type with rhythm and likely supply money.
10 Silly Stacey will defy the property systems daily.
11 The yield for the policy was forty or fifty daily.
```

LOCATE THE G KEY

F→G

The G is keyed with the F finger. Place your fingers on the home keys and practice the reach to G.

```
fgf fgf fgf fgf
```

PRACTICE THE G KEY REACH

Use proper technique.

Key each line two times.

1 fgf fgf tugs go dog tog fog got gear good goat hag
2 page high again filing gentle flight college legal
3 sign glasses gadget pledge adjust refuge glad page
4 budget sprung urgent program oxygen angry again go
5 The dogs will not growl at the great green trucks.
6 My good agreement will not get a good arrangement.
7 Granted, great arrangement would get good golfing.
8 The college program took three gifted giant gains.
9 Gene will judge the urgency of the budget, George.
10 Gale was going to adjust and judge the oxygen gas.
11 Guy will adjust the pledge for all yearly exports.

INCREASE KEYING SPEED

Race to beat the computer and increase your speed.

Key each line two times.

1 In the future, people will use computers each day.
2 Most new business transactions might occur orally.
3 Net expenses for the past month are on the tables.
4 I wished that annual land leases were not illegal.
5 The Feds blocked the bid for all yields for taxes.
6 New employee styles are good and can yield yearly.
7 Big red fish can be tracked with future computers.
8 You need two business transactions for generosity.
9 Paula expedited the budget policy for the company.
10 The angry judge pledged to grant the urgent price.

□□□□1□□□□2□□□□3□□□□4□□□□5□□□□6□□□□7□□□□8□□□□9□□□10

Measure Progress

Take two 1-minute timings.

Minimum goal: 16 wam

Try to reach a new speed goal.

1 My annual family days taken were not too exciting.

2 Public bids for federal lands are considered good.

3 Many corporate business transactions are exciting.

1 2 3 4 5 6 7 8 9 10

End-of-Lesson Procedure

At the end of each lesson, you will have the following options:

1. To restart the same lesson, press the F1 function key.
2. To return to the Lessons Menu, press ESC. This action automatically will save the completed lesson.
3. To proceed to the next, or any other lesson, highlight your choice on the menu and press Enter.
4. To return to the Main Menu, press ESC again.
5. To print the lesson, select Print Activities.
6. To exit the program:
   a. Select the Exit option and press Enter.
   b. When the DOS prompt appears on the screen, remove your data disk.
   c. Turn off the monitor. (Your instructor also may ask you to turn off the computer and printer.)

10

V, Z, Diagonal, and Question Mark Keys

GOALS

- Reinforce Previous Learning
- Learn New Keys V, Z, Diagonal, and Question Mark
- Increase Keying Speed

Remember the "Get Ready" checklist.

REVIEW

```
sws sws juj juj ;p; ;p; sxs sxs jyj jyj fgf fgf gy
Xerox xray extra excellent excess expand next flax
Ugly physical weary physicians unduly photography,
The employee taxes yielded gross percentage yield.
Guy had excise taxes and good agreements for sale.
```

LOCATE THE V KEY

Use correct finger position.

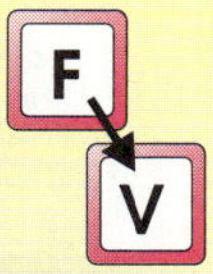

The V is keyed with the F finger. Place your fingers on the home keys and practice the reach to V.

```
fvf fvf fvf fvf
```

Practice the V Key Reach

Keep your fingers curved.

Key each line two times.

1 fvf fvf very vain vacant vacations vaccine vex vat
2 via even travel advise review seven private versus
3 arrival adverse advertise understand view division
4 visitors vocational waiver vault convenience seven
5 available waiver advise advertise vocational vault
6 The average vote has value. I vied for vice jobs.
7 Vic and Victoria have a very vain view of victory.
8 It is not vain to get a vaccine before a vacation.
9 Please review the division advertisement for Vera.
10 The arrival of the vocational visitors was urgent.
11 Please understand the inconvenience of the waiver.

Locate the Z Key

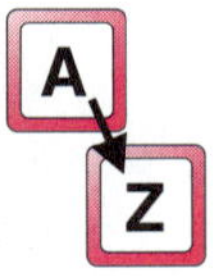

The Z is keyed with the A finger. Place your fingers on the home keys and practice the reach to Z.

aza aza aza aza

Practice the Z Key Reach

As you key the Z, your S finger may lift slightly.

Key each line two times.

1 aza aza azalea azure Aztec buzz lizard zipper zoos
2 raze whiz citizen seize minimize recognize analyze
3 amaze hazard freeze bazaar zigzag organize itemize
4 lazy crazy hazy prize minimize zeal size raze whiz
5 Zebra zeal size jazz zip lazy freeze zero citizens
6 The fuzzy and zany lizard zipped by the zoo zones.
7 It was good to zealously zero in on frozen ozones.
8 Zelda analyzed the prizes from the citizen bazaar.
9 Itemize the dozen tax hazards for the whiz, Lizzy.
10 Buzz authorized a new text for the next tax class.
11 Those citizens voted to waive the division bazaar.

Locate the ?/ Key

A diagonal or slash (/) is used between letters in some abbreviations, between the numbers in a fraction, and between certain interchangeable expressions, such as and/or. No space is left before or after a diagonal.

The / (diagonal) is keyed with the ; finger. Place your fingers on the home keys and practice the reach to /.

;/; ;/; ;/; ;/;

Remember: Do not space before or after the diagonal.

Practice the ?/ Key Reach

Key each line two times.

1 ;/ ;/ ;/ either/or neither/nor or/for his/her a/an
2 yes/no high/low pass/fail right/wrong up/down a/an
3 My pass/fail rule was not his/her in/out decision.

Locate the ?/ Key

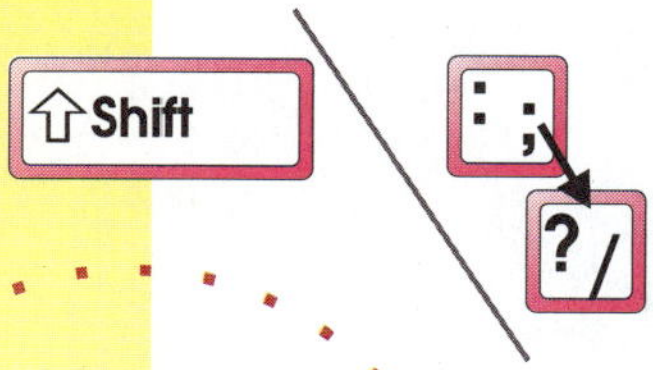

A question mark is used at the end of direct questions. Use two spaces after the question mark.

The ? is the shift of the / and is keyed with the ; finger. Place your fingers on the home keys and practice the reach to ?.

;?; ;?; ;?; ;?;

Practice the ?/ Key Reach

Key each line two times.

1 ;?; ;?; Did you buzz? Who is it? Whose vacation?
2 Where is our new pen? Have you seen Tex? Who me?
3 What is going on here? Why do they work? Pamela?
4 Will they come? Has Kim called? Where was Henry?
5 When will Vic get home? Where was that prize bag?
6 Why did Lacy waive the decision? Where is George?
7 What did the prize advertisement reveal to Walter?
8 How did Yvonne organize the items for convenience?
9 What were the pass/fail rates for the examination?
10 Will Irene become the new class computer whiz kid?

Space twice after a question mark at the end of a sentence.

Increase Keying Speed

Key each line two times.

Try to reach a new speed goal.

Remember: Space twice after a question mark.

1 The vulture was a vulgar, vigorous big black bird.
2 It became evident when that vapor rose from a vat.
3 Our frozen and frizzy red dog walks like a zombie.
4 Vera and Vic have a very bad vain view of history.
5 Many business transactions occur at our new house.
6 Zelda, an irate citizen, organized a crazy bazaar.
7 The pass/fail rules were his/her yes/no decisions.
8 He/she decided one in/out motion was not a yes/no.
9 Where is the house? Is he in? What was it? Why?
10 Who took the letter? What did she say? Who said?
□□□□1□□□□2□□□□3□□□□4□□□□5□□□□6□□□□7□□□□8□□□□9□□□10

Measure Progress

Take two 1-minute timings.

Minimum goal: 17 wam

Try to exceed the minimum goal.

1 A chip technology allows less expensive computers.
2 The average vote has values. How did Jan find me?
3 Our exercise programs are needed for good muscles.
□□□□1□□□□2□□□□3□□□□4□□□□5□□□□6□□□□7□□□□8□□□□9□□□10

End-of-Lesson Procedure

At the end of each lesson, you will have the following options:

1. To restart the same lesson, press the F1 function key.
2. To return to the Lessons Menu, press ESC.
3. To proceed to the next, or any other lesson, highlight your choice on the menu and press Enter.
4. To return to the Main Menu, press ESC again.
5. To print the lesson, select Print Activities.
6. To exit the program:
   a. Select the Exit option and press Enter.
   b. When the DOS prompt appears on the screen, remove your data disk.
   c. Turn off the monitor. (Your instructor also may ask you to turn off the computer and printer.)

11

Q, Hyphen, and Tab Keys

GOALS

- Reinforce Previous Learning
- Learn New Keys Q, Hyphen, and Tab
- Learn Word Wrap

Review

Key each line twice.

Use proper technique.

```
1 sxs sxs jyj jyj fgf fgf fvf fvf aza aza ;/; ;?; ;?
2 Was that public bid for the old federal land high?
3 That new pass/fail system was his/her new bid too.
4 Was it difficult to realize that ozone is not hot?
5 Janet indicated that something extra could happen.
```

Locate the Q Key

The Q is keyed with the A finger. Place your fingers on the home keys and practice the reach to Q.

```
aqa aqa aqa aqa
```

PRACTICE THE Q KEY REACH

Key each line two times.

1 aqa aqa aqua aquanaut aquariums aquatics equal aqa
2 quick quiet query quart delinquent adequate quorum
3 quota quality quire unique quantity request acquit
4 acquire inquire quotient antique quit quality quay
5 The question of the quiet quest was for the Queen.
6 Their quart is a quantity that must be questioned.
7 A question concerning the Queen was quietly posed.
8 The unique antique qualified as the quality quota.
9 Quint will acquire an adequate quantity of quilts.
10 Inquire about the delinquent quotas acquired Quan.
11 Did that quota require equal distribution of ages?

Try to keep your wrist still as you key the Q.

LOCATE THE - KEY

Hyphens are used to form compound adjectives, nouns, and verbs. Hyphens help readers understand that a combination of words has a single meaning, such as state-of-the-art software. Hyphens also show the division of syllables in a word, such as knowl-edge. The dash (--) is used in informal writing to introduce or summarize information. Dashes also may be used to set off information from the rest of the sentence. Dashes are constructed of two hyphens. Do not insert a space between the hyphen or dash and the characters that come before or after it.

The - (hyphen) is keyed with the ; finger. Place your fingers on the home keys and practice the reach to -.

;-; ;-; ;-; ;-;

PRACTICE THE - KEY REACH

Key each line two times.

```
1 ;-; ;-; ;-; self-concepts up-to-date part-time ;-;
2 His new mother-in-law gave him a part-time salary.
3 My part-time work requires up-to-date information.
4 Their resignation--not mine--begins tomorrow, Hal.
5 Newer negotiations--dated as of May--were resumed.
```

Remember: A dash is keyed as two hyphens.

LEARN TO USE THE Tab KEY

When keying information, sometimes it is necessary to indent paragraphs or arrange text or data in columns. Tab settings allow you to move quickly to predetermined stops across the display screen and thus save time for many applications. Most microcomputer software packages have present tabs called **default tabs.** In this software program, one default tab is set at five spaces from the left margin. When the cursor is at the left margin, striking the Tab key will indent that line five spaces, the normal paragraph indentation. Other software programs may have different default settings.

Most word-processing programs also allow you to change default tabs or set new tab stops. You will learn how to change tab settings in this program in a later lesson. Until that lesson, you will use the Tab key only to indent the first line of a paragraph.

LOCATE THE Tab KEY

Strike Tab to indent a paragraph.

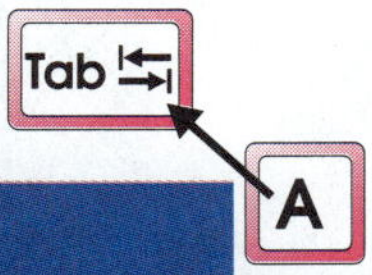

The Tab key is located to the left of the Q key and is struck with the A finger. The other fingers should remain in home key position. Place your fingers on the home keys. Practice striking the Tab key.

```
a    a    a    a    a    a    a    a ↵
  ↑    ↑    ↑    ↑    ↑    ↑    ↑
 tab  tab  tab  tab  tab  tab  tab
```

Learn Automatic Word Wrap

Most word processing and microcomputer programs include an automatic "word wrap" feature. When a word is too long to fit within the established right margin, word wrap automatically will carry that word down to begin a new line at the left margin. With this feature, the operator needs to strike Enter only at the end of short lines and at the end of a paragraph. Word wrap is an efficient, time-saving feature for the operator.

In this program, word wrap will be on for any paragraph drill and for all composition and formatting exercises. Continue to strike Enter at the end of one-line drills only.

Practice the Tab Key Reach and Word Wrap

Using the default Tab setting of five spaces, strike the Tab key to indent the following paragraphs. Key each paragraph one time. Strike Enter only at the end of each paragraph.

Strike Enter to end a paragraph.

```
     Your order for a copy of the software program was received today.  The order will be shipped Monday.
     Please notify us as soon as you receive the shipment.  An invoice will be included.
     For additional information and service, please contact us.  We appreciate your business.
```

Practice Tabs in Paragraph Copy

Key each paragraph two times. Read the copy from the book and key the lines on the computer. Strike Enter only at the end of each paragraph.

```
     An exercise/fitness program is essential for your muscle tone.  The in-service training will be effective if the proper techniques/methods are used.  Part-time application will not work.  Are there any questions?  Do you wish to begin?
     Many students like the pass/fail system.  It is an up-to-date approach to grading.  Your decision about pass/fail courses needs to be made as enrollment--not payment--starts tomorrow.
```

Measure Progress

Starting with this lesson, all Measure Progress paragraphs will begin with a standard five-space indentation. Press the Tab key to indent each paragraph. Word wrap will be turned on automatically so you should not strike Enter except to end the paragraph.

Also, each paragraph is rated according to its syllabic intensity (S.I.). Syllabic intensity is one measure of the difficulty of the copy. The higher the syllabic intensity, the more difficult the copy.

Minimum goal: 18 wam
1.4 S.I.

Take two 1-minute timings. Word wrap is active.

Now that you have learned to use the alphabetic keyboard, you will begin learning the numeric keys. As you progress, your speed will increase slowly until you have reached your goal of quick and correct keyboarding. At the end of this lesson, you should be averaging at least eighteen words per minute.

1 2 3 4 5 6 7 8 9 10

End-of-Lesson Procedure

At the end of each lesson, you will have the following options:

1. To restart the same lesson, press the F1 function key.
2. To return to the Lessons Menu, press ESC. This action automatically will save the completed lesson.
3. To proceed to the next, or any other lesson, highlight your choice on the menu and press Enter.
4. To return to the Main Menu, press ESC again.
5. To print the lesson, select Print Activities.
6. To exit the program:
   a. Select the Exit option and press Enter.
   b. When the DOS prompt appears on the screen, remove your data disk.
   c. Turn off the monitor. (Your instructor also may ask you to turn off the computer and printer.)

12 Skill Building

GOALS

- Reinforce Previous Learning
- Increase Keying Speed
- Improve Keying Accuracy
- Learn Backspace-Key Correction Method

REVIEW

Key each line two times.

1 We saw seven very fat birds and photographed them.
2 The judges told the boys to fix the broken window.
3 The six zeros on my bad check were quietly erased.
4 Queens were not too excited about a voting frenzy.
5 Sometimes a good argument can obtain sure success.

INCREASE KEYING SPEED

Key and space quickly.

Key each line two times.

1 he in on so or of it at if be by ti do ha la it or
2 if it is or no an so in as at no up me en an of on
3 how cut big put hot ten lie was per its eve cab do
4 too for bag him did gas get out fly old bug cat as
5 was the/are you/and the/was all/can she/let go of/
1 2 3 4 5 6 7 8 9 10

IMPROVE KEYING ACCURACY—REVIEW ALL KEYS LEARNED

The following drill serves three purposes. First, the drill lines review all alphabetic keys learned. Second, speed achievement for each line is analyzed and reported. Finally, accuracy of key strokes for each line is analyzed and reported.

For the following exercise, key each line. Strike Enter at the end of the line. Look at the screen. Your speed performance is reported as words a minute (wam). Your accuracy performance is reported as total errors in the line. Words that contain errors also are highlighted so you can find them easily. Note your performance on the first attempt. Then key the same line a second time. Compare the results of each attempt.

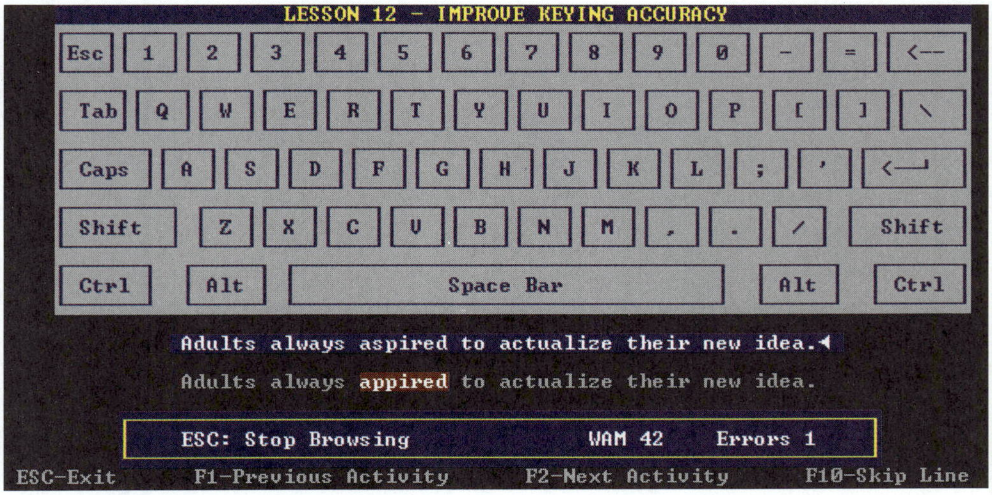

At this point, your goal is to key each line at an average speed of 18 wam with no more than two errors. If you are meeting the speed goal but have more than two errors, you may have to slow down slightly to gain accuracy. If you are not meeting the speed goal, you may want to repeat the Increase Keying Speed and Measure Progress drills in Lessons 6-11 before completing this lesson. Then return to this drill to reevaluate your progress.

After keying this exercise if you are meeting or exceeding both the speed and accuracy goals, proceed to the remaining activities in this lesson.

Minimum goal: 18 wam with no more than 2 errors per line

1 Adults always aspired to actualize their new idea.
2 Beware of bogus business battles that boost sales.
3 Careless careening cars caused a curious accident.
4 Did the untimely death of David Duncans deter her?
5 Ira easily sees that errors erase earnest efforts.
6 Family is the happy foundation of future fortunes.
7 Great Roger Greson generates good press greetings.
8 How will Hank Howel heat the homes for the hungry?
9 Will it be filled? Who will fill it? She did it.
10 Jack, Joe, and Julie jabbered and jumped jauntily.

Practice correct techniques.

Try to exceed the minimum goals.

11 Knowing how to knit crazy kits was good knowledge.
12 Free lands are like the lighting of liberty lamps.
13 A major machine can match the main and major mass.
14 Note the new number of major novels that are sold.
15 Oil spills in the ocean are offensive for oysters.
16 A pinch of pepper was put on top of the four pots.
17 Quality questions are quite quaint to Queen Betsy.
18 She was the real reason I refused to receive Raye.
19 Setting sail is serious business to salty sailors.
20 My tried technical technique was true to the text.
21 Use the unions to unite those usual loading units.
22 Vic valued the valves as the vapor rose from vats.
23 Where was that wall wanted when this war was over?
24 Excise taxes are taxing on the extra external tax.
25 If you look closely you will yearn for yummy yams.
26 A ZIP code may speed your dizzy letter to the zoo.

Learn Backspace-Key Correction Method

Often you will recognize misstrokes as you are keying. These can be corrected immediately using the Backspace key.

The Backspace key is located at the far right on the top row of the keyboard. It is keyed with the right little finger. When pressed, the Backspace key moves back one space and deletes the character in that space. If the cursor is at the left margin, pressing the Backspace key will move it to the line above.

To practice using the Backspace key, complete the following:

1. Key the words `the program` but do not press Enter.
2. Using the semicolon finger, backspace four times. Notice that the characters `gram` are deleted.
3. Key `blem.` (Again, do not press Enter).
4. Notice that you have changed the *program* to the *problem*.

From now on, you can use the Backspace key during most composition and document formatting exercises. In addition, if your instructor wants the Backspace key to be available to you during a Measure Progress drill, you can activate it by selecting "Options" at the Main Menu. The following screen will appear:

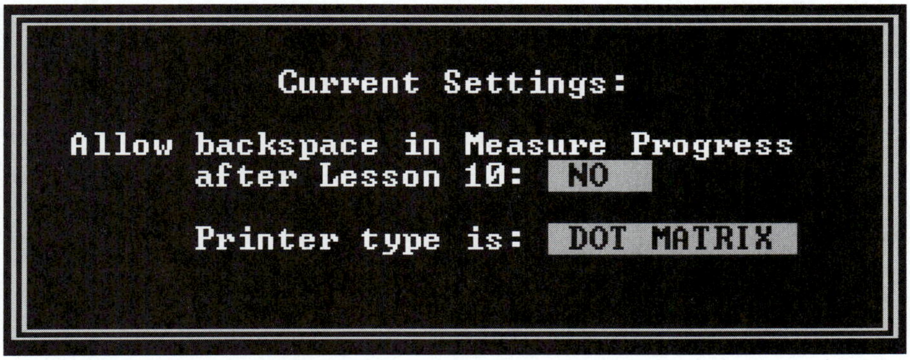

Remember: Turn on Backspace if instructed to do so.

When the program is first loaded, the Backspace setting defaults to "no." To activate Backspace, press the F6 function key. Look at the screen. Notice that "no" is replaced with "yes."

To change back to "no" again, press the F5 function key. The last option selected will remain as the default setting until changed. All Measure Progress drills completed with Backspace on will be marked so that you will know that this option was activated.

Note: The Backspace option is not available in Review, Practice, Increase Keying Speed, or Improve Keying Accuracy drills.

Measure Progress

Take two 1-minute timings.

Minimum goal: 19 wam with four or fewer errors 1.6 S.I.

Key quickly.

```
     Computers are very important and valuable in our lives today.  It is essential that we all become familiar with this wonderful tool.  If you want to become computer literate, you must have some knowledge about computers and their operation.  Also, you should have some experience using the computer.
```

1 2 3 4 5 6 7 8 9 10

End-of-Lesson Procedure

At the end of each lesson, you will have the following options:

1. To restart the same lesson, press the F1 function key.
2. To return to the Lessons Menu, press ESC. This action automatically will save the completed lesson.
3. To proceed to the next, or any other lesson, highlight your choice on the menu and press Enter.
4. To return to the Main Menu, press ESC again.
5. To print the lesson, select Print Activities.
6. To exit the program:
    a. Select the Exit option and press Enter.
    b. When the DOS prompt appears on the screen, remove your data disk.
    c. Turn off the monitor. (Your instructor also may ask you to turn off the computer and printer.)

UNIT 2-
TOP-ROW NUMBERS/SYMBOLS

13 1, 5, and 0 Keys

GOALS

- Reinforce Previous Learning
- Learn New Keys 1, 5, and 0
- Learn Number-Reading Techniques
- Understand Speed vs. Accuracy Development

Remember the "Get Ready" checklist.

Review

Key each line two times.

1 Joe was excited about having a quiet meal with Oz.

2 He saw Tim fly. Who was Rochell talking to today?

3 How many computers were ordered with green tables?

4 The survey is systematic and typical of Jo and me.

5 Their excited dogs bit the quiet small calico cat.

Locate the ! 1 Key

Keep your fingers in home key position so you don't lose your place.

The 1 is keyed with the A finger. Place your fingers on the home keys and practice the reach to 1.

aq1a aq1a aq1a aq1a

Practice the !1 Key Reach

Be sure to key the numeral 1 (one), not the letter l (el).

Key each line two times.

1 aq1a aq1a aq1a aq1a a1a a1a 11 ask 111 and 11 a1a1

2 11 at 111 ad 11 air 11.111 as 111,11 attire 1a1 at

3 His mailing address was 1 North Elmsquares Avenue.

4 The appointments were on 1/11, 1/1 and 11/1, Mark.

5 Please send me 111 orders of Number 1,111 pencils.

Keep your eyes on the copy.

Locate the %5 Key

The 5 is keyed with the F finger. Place your fingers on the home keys and practice the reach to 5.

fr5f fr5f fr5f fr5f

Practice the %5 Key Reach

Key each line two times.

1 fr5f fr5f fr5f f5f f5f 5 55 555 555 5555 fast 5.5

2 555 fire 55,5 for 55 fan 55 far 5555 fast 5.55 of

3 Send 55 of the first 155 tickets you receive now.

4 The record indicated on 5/1/51 she was born here.

5 The 15 girls visited all 51 sites on February 15.

When keying the numeral 5, keep your other fingers in home key position.

Locate the)0 Key

When keying the numeral 0, keep your J finger in home key position.

The 0 is keyed with the ; finger. Place your fingers on the home keys and practice the reach to 0.

;p0; ;p0; ;p0; ;p0;

Practice the)0 Key Reach

Be sure to key the numeral 0 (zero), not the letter O (oh).

Key each line two times.

1 ;p0; ;p0; ;p0; ;0; ;0; ;0; 00 000 ;000; 00 ;or; 0;

2 00 was 000 and; 00.00 ;the; 00 for 0.00 or 00 old.

3 5 0 50 01 05 050 511 510 150 015 01.50 0.015 50 .5

4 af; 150; ;fa 051 fa; 510 a;f 105 ;af 015 5101; 500

5 Contact 501-5010 if you need 50 additional yachts.

Learn Number-Reading Techniques

To key numbers more efficiently, practice the following number-reading techniques:

1. For one-digit numbers, say the number to yourself as you key it.
   Example: 5 Say five.
2. For two-digit numbers, say the number as a unit.
   Example: 55 Say fifty-five.
3. For three-digit numbers, say the first digit as a separate unit and the other two as a unit.
   Example: 511 Say five/eleven.
   Example: 555 Say five/fifty-five.

4. For four-digit numbers, say the first two digits as a unit and then the last two as a unit.

   Example: 5511 Say fifty-five/eleven.

   Example: 5555 Say fifty-five/fifty-five.

5. For five-digit numbers, say the first two digits as a unit followed by a group of three.

   Example: 51155 Say fifty-one/one fifty-five.

   Example: 11555 Say eleven/five fifty-five.

6. If the numbers have other characters included in them, read the character as a separate unit and then continue with the pattern.

   Example: 1,111 Say one/comma/one eleven.

   Example: 238-58-9423 Say two thirty-eight/hyphen/fifty-eight/hyphen/ninety-four/twenty-three.

Do not become too concerned if you notice a speed drop in your performance when keying numbers and symbols. As you practice the upper-row reaches, speed performance will increase.

Understand Speed vs. Accuracy

Remember: Concentrate on speed or accuracy.

As you develop keyboarding skills, your progress is reported both in terms of speed (wam) and accuracy (number of errors). However, speed and accuracy should be practiced separately. When you are keying for speed, you should key as quickly as possible without concern for keying errors. To reach new speed goals, you probably will exceed suggested error limits. Once you reach a new speed goal, you can decrease your keying rate slightly to bring the number of errors you make back within the suggested error limits. The rule of thumb is: Increase your keying speed first; then control speed to improve your accuracy.

In this program, "Increase Keying Speed" drills emphasize speed development. "Improve Keying Accuracy" drills emphasize control or accuracy. If you do not reach the accuracy goal, repeat the line.

Always decide on only one goal—speed or accuracy. Do not attempt to accomplish both at the same time.

Increase Keying Speed

Only speed is analyzed and reported.

Key and space quickly.

```
1 of at or in an it if is to te ti do id di my fa go
2 an is he at me go bo as of it an am co to if at it
3 say day aim big way hat dim sit sin bet did war go
4 won all bar eat did cat ton saw tar vat was zip an
5 then sign half lake lens hand fish then than hands
    1    2    3    4    5    6    7    8    9   10
```

Improve Keying Accuracy

Both speed and accuracy are analyzed and reported.

Minimum goal: 17 wam

Try to exceed the minimum goal.

```
1 stall eggs hill tall flee need teen seed feed sell
2 kiss less heel knee hall fell add need skill shall
3 glee little indeed likeness allied settling assess
4 skiing lessen haggle feeling endless stiff gallant
5 egg install fiddle assist attend falling attendant
6 Edward came to work on 1/15/05 and left on 5/1/05.
7 51 015 050 1155 5500 15100 10015 5000 501550 5.055
8 My new ZIP code is 15100.  Janey lost 15.5 pounds.
9 Call me at 510-5501.  Is her number 510151-001550?
10 Please send our letters of 5/5/15 and 11/5/05 now.
```

Measure Progress

Take two 1-minute timings.

Minimum goal: 20 wam with four or fewer errors 1.3 S.I.

```
1      Where are the new orders?  We must fill them as
2 soon as possible.  The only way we can be competitive
3 is to fill our orders faster than the other
4 companies.  If there is a problem, we must all pitch
5 in and work overtime.  Of course, you will be paid
6 time-and-a-half for all overtime.
    1    2    3    4    5    6    7    8    9   10
```

END-OF-LESSON PROCEDURE

At the end of each lesson, you will have the following options:

1. To restart the same lesson, press the F1 function key.
2. To return to the Lessons Menu, press ESC. This action automatically will save the completed lesson.
3. To proceed to the next, or any other lesson, highlight your choice and press Enter.
4. To return to the Main Menu, press ESC again.
5. To print the lesson, select Print Activities.
6. To exit the program:
    a. Select the Exit option and press Enter.
    b. When the DOS prompt appears on the screen, remove your data disk.
    c. Turn off the monitor. (Your instructor also may ask you to turn off the computer and printer.)

14

3, 7, and 9 Keys

GOALS

- Reinforce Previous Learning
- Learn New Keys 3, 7, and 9
- Learn to Identify Errors
- Learn to Edit, Add, and Delete Copy

REVIEW

Remember the "Get Ready" checklist.

Key each line two times.

1 Zero is the winning prize number of quality gifts.

2 The two red tables ordered yesterday just arrived.

3 Texx purchased oil wells instead of topaz jewelry.

4 Al, 1 foot, 15 dogs, 10 nos. My code is 5151; 50.

5 Volume 15, page 51 states that his age was not 51.

6 The order included: 15150 desks and 10151 chairs.

LOCATE THE #3 KEY

Practice reading numbers in units.

The 3 is keyed with the D finger. Place your fingers on the home keys and practice the reach to 3.

de3d de3d de3d de3d

Practice the #3 Key Reach

Key each line two times.

When you key 33, say thirty-three.

1 de3d de3d de3d de3d d3d d3d 3 33 333 33 33 d3 d3d3
2 33 did 333 dare 33 debut 33 dorm 33 door 3333 dark
3 3 1 31 3 5 35 3 0 30 33 13 31 53 35 30 03 303 35.3
4 It is 3:33, so send number 3 to check the lid now.
5 The list included checks 13, 33, 35, 351, 153, 30.

Locate the &7 Key

The 7 is keyed with the J finger. Place your fingers on the home keys and practice the reach to 7.

ju7j ju7j ju7j ju7j

Practice the &7 Key Reach

Key each line two times.

1 ju7j ju7j ju7j ju7j j7j j7j j7j j7j 7 77 7j7j 77j7
2 77 jar 77 job 77 jacks 77 jam 77 jip 77 jeer 7 jaw
3 7 1 71 7 5 75 7 3 73 7 0 70 1/75 1/37 7/37 7/ 75.7
4 Your letter of 7/31/75 included 13 of the 75 here.
5 Order 77 was for 37, 73, 75, 70, 17, 707, and 757.

LOCATE THE (9 KEY

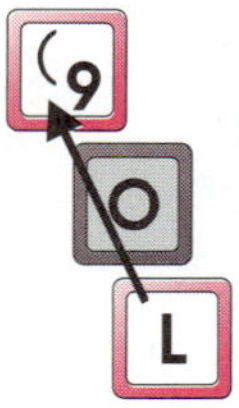

The 9 is keyed with the L finger. Place your fingers on the home keys and practice the reach to 9.

```
lo9l lo9l lo9l lo9l
```

PRACTICE THE (9 KEY REACH

Key each line two times.

Numeral 1, not letter l.

```
1 lo9l lo9l lo9l lo9l l9l l9l 9 9 9 99 9.99 9.9 99.9
2 99 lift 99 low 99 law 99 lure 99 lake 99 look 9999
3 9 1 91 9 7 97 9 3 93 9 5 95 9 0 90 1/99 9/9/9 9779
4 Jimmy sent 33, Sally 79, Kent 95, and Judith 3579.
5 The total invoice was:  99, 97, 93, 95, 90, and 9.
```

INCREASE KEYING SPEED

Note: Spaces are used with diagonals here only to emphasize the phrases.

Only speed is analyzed and reported.

```
1 if it /it is /as is /as it /if he /if in /in it
2 of it /do it /it is /as it /at us /of so /so he
3 art bug cat dud eat far fox had ill fog sap tow
4 non mud out son jar joy gad its but box toy pay
5 ant lake had the sign half disk lane tame eight
    1    2    3    4    5    6    7    8    9   10
```

Improve Keying Accuracy

Key with control—no more than one error per line. Repeat a line if necessary.

Both speed and accuracy are analyzed and reported.

```
1 The green cathode ray tube is used for displaying.
2 Down time is when the computer is not functioning.
3 Visible and vigorous exercise is viewed as worthy.
4 My last letter of 11/17/97 was mailed at 9:53 p.m.
5 That length of time was 39 minutes and 59 seconds.
6 Call 379-993-7937 and order 97 folders and 7 pens.
```

Learn to Identify Errors

Even though the software for this program will identify your keying errors in many exercises, it is an important skill to be able to proofread copy. In some activities, you will need to identify errors by marking them on the printout. In other activities, you will need to identify and correct errors on the screen.

Use this guideline when identifying errors in printed copy:

Count only one error per word. If errors occur in the punctuation and spacing that follow a word, count the word as one error.

Study the following paragraph to see how keying errors are counted. There are eight errors in the paragraph.

```
     Computers ate very imtorpant and valuable in out
lives today. It is esssential that weall become
familiar with this wonderful tool, If you want to
become computer literate, you must have some
knolwedge about computers and their operation. Alsо,
you should have some experience using the computer.
After identifying errors, the copy should be
corrected. In some cases, all the material must be
keyed again. With word-processing software, however,
most corrections can be made within the copy already
keyed.
```

LEARN TO EDIT COPY

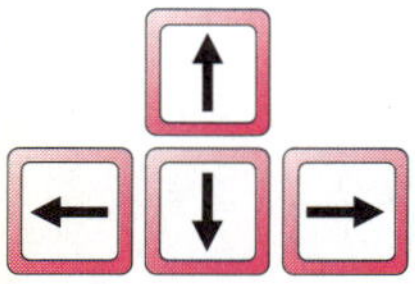

Once a document has been entered, it can be edited on-screen by using the Cursor Movement (Arrow) keys to move to the spot where a correction is needed. These keys are located either as a separate cluster of keys located between the alphabetic keyboard and the 10-key keypad or on the 10-key numeric keypad. Look at your keyboard to determine the location of the Cursor Movement keys.

When these keys are pressed, the cursor moves in the direction indicated by the arrow—left, right, up, or down.

Now do the following:

1. Key this paragraph.

```
     Selling is a skill and an art.  You can learn
the skills, but the unique application of those
skills is an art form.
```

2. Practice using the Arrow keys by doing the following:

   Move the cursor under the `r` in `art`.

   Move the cursor to the right under the `n` in `learn`.

   Move the cursor down under the `q` in `unique`.

   Move the cursor to the left under the `u` in `but`.

Practice moving the cursor to other locations until you are comfortable with the procedure.

Before printing a document, you should proofread it on the screen. Use the Arrow keys to move to the beginning of a document. Then use the Down-Arrow key to scroll through the document as you proof it for errors.

Once you have printed a document, you should proof the printed copy for errors you may have missed.

When keying composition and application documents, you will be able to move the cursor to any location within the document. You will then be able to insert or delete text if you desire. You will not be able to use the Arrow keys during drills or Measure Progress activities.

Learn to Add and Delete Copy

When you identify errors in copy that already has been keyed, you can correct the copy before printing. In some software programs, you can replace the incorrect characters by keying over them. In other software programs, you must first delete the incorrect character and then key the correct character. In this program, you can insert characters at the cursor position. If you are changing an incorrect character, it is best to delete the incorrect character first and then key the correct character.

Practice adding/inserting characters by doing the following:

1. Key `Micrcompiter Fornating` exactly as shown with the errors.
2. Identify the keying errors in the words.
3. Move the cursor under the second *c* in `Micrcompiter.`
4. Key `o`. Notice that the *o* is inserted in the proper place and the cursor moves under the *c*. To add omitted text, you move the cursor to the character to the right of the point where you wish to add text, and key the omitted character. It is then inserted.
5. Move the cursor under the *t* in `Fornating.`
6. Key `t`. The new character is inserted.

To delete or correct a character:

1. Move the cursor under the *i* in `compiter`. Before you can key the correct character, you must delete the *i*. With the cursor under the *i*, press the Delete key. Notice that the *i* is removed from the screen and the text automatically moves over to fill in the space. Now key `u`. Remember: If you have unwanted characters, you must delete them using the Delete key before keying the correct character.
2. Use the Delete key to delete the incorrect character in `Fornatting`. Then insert the proper character so that the word is correct.
3. Remember: You also can use the Backspace key to delete incorrect characters. Position your cursor at the end of the word `Formatting.` Backspace two times. Notice that a character is removed each time you backspace. Now key the correct characters again.
4. Practice adding, deleting, and backspacing until you are comfortable with these editing keys.

You will be able to use these editing keys only in the composition and word-processor activities.

Minimum goal: 21 wam with four or fewer errors 1.5 S.I.

Try to exceed the minimum goal.

Measure Progress

Take two 1-minute timings.

In word processing, duplicating means to copy. In order to copy data from the monitor screen, you must follow the copy instructions in your computer manual or software program. Copy is a BASIC language command. If you want hard copy or print copy of your work, you will use the print instructions or print command.

There are times when the computer is not functioning properly. This time is called down time. Down time may hamper production schedules.

1 2 3 4 5 6 7 8 9 10

End-of-Lesson Procedure

At the end of each lesson, you will have the following options:

1. To restart the same lesson, press the F1 function key.
2. To return to the Lessons Menu, press ESC. This action automatically will save the completed lesson.
3. To proceed to the next, or any other lesson, highlight your choice on the menu and press Enter.
4. To return to the Main Menu, press ESC again.
5. To print the lesson, select Print Activities.
6. To exit the program:
   a. Select the Exit option and press Enter.
   b. When the DOS prompt appears on the screen, remove your data disk.
   c. Turn off the monitor. (Your instructor also may ask you to turn off the computer and printer.)

15

2, 4, 6, and 8 Keys

GOALS

- Reinforce Previous Learning
- Learn New Keys 2, 4, 6, and 8
- Learn to Name, Save, Print, and Retrieve a Document
- Practice Composition Skills

REVIEW

Remember the "Get Ready" checklist.

Key each line two times.

```
1 An author is an originator of the stored document.
2 Store my computer documents on the storage medium.
3 Raze the yellow building for luxury prize hazards.
4 Rob asked Sara to keyboard the letter by 7:39 p.m.
5 Were the 9730 items not delivered on 10/1 at 3:09?
6 Orders 79, 30, 91, 15, 59, 13, 157, 173 are ready.
7 Please send tickets 973, 591, 715, 309, 510, 5170.
```

When you key 7:39, say seven/colon/thirty-nine.

LOCATE THE @2 KEY

The 2 is keyed with the S finger.

```
sw2s sw2s sw2s sw2s
```

Practice the @2 Key Reach

Key each line two times.

Keep your fingers curved.

1 sw2s sw2s sw2s sw2s s2s s2s s2s s2s 2 22 saw 22.22

2 22 silly 22 shoe 22 skirt 22 sure 222 sat 22.2 set

3 2 1 21 2 0 20 2 5 25 22 23 2/35 5/22 1/22 21/25 22

4 Flight 72 left at 2:27 on 2/2/92. It is 2:32 a.m.

5 These missing items are 201, 129, 723, 91, and 20.

Locate the $4 Key

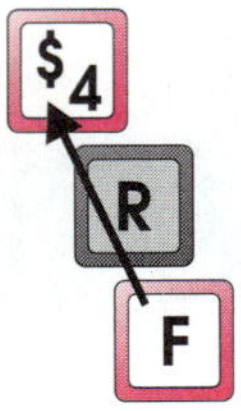

The 4 is keyed with the F finger.

fr4f fr4f fr4f fr4f

Practice the $4 Key Reach

Key each line two times.

When keying the numeral 4, keep the A finger in home key position.

1 fr4f fr4f fr4f fr4f f4f f4f f4f 44 four 44 far 444

2 44 fire 44 free 444 fore 44 file 444 fold 44.4 fig

3 4 1 41 4 2 42 4 5 45 4 0 40 1 44 14 1/44 4/41 4/40

4 My order arrived on 4/4/94. A gross is 144 items.

5 Please check these items: 40, 42, 24, 14, and 45.

Locate the ^6 Key

The 6 is keyed with the J finger.

ju6j ju6j ju6j ju6j

Practice the ^6 Key Reach

When keying the numeral 6, keep the ; finger in home key position.

Key each line two times.

1 ju6j ju6j ju6j ju6j j6j j6j j6j j6j 6 66 66.6 6/66

2 6 jar 66 juice 66 jury 66 janitor 66 judge 666 jam

3 6 66 6 1 61 6 5 65 6 4 64 6 3 63 56 0 60 466 76756

4 The computer compared 646 items with 626 criteria.

5 Ticket sales for 6, 65, 61, 16, 676 were reported.

Locate the *8 Key

The 8 is keyed with the K finger.

ki8k ki8k ki8k ki8k

Practice the *8 Key Reach

Key each line two times.

1 ki8k ki8k ki8k ki8k k8k k8k k8k k8k 8 88 8.88 .808
2 88 kite 88 kidney 88 kettle 888 kazoos 888.88 keys
3 8 88 884 886 883 388 588 288 881 2/82 28/850 14/85
4 It was 8:38 p.m. when my piece of luggage arrived.
5 Sales in 1987 increased by 86, 84, 80, 181, or 27.

Increase Keying Speed

Note: Spaces are used with the diagonals to emphasize the phrases.

Only speed is analyzed and reported.

1 to it /at up /to no /in my /do it so /on it /do a
2 by my /on it /is no /in so /so it is /as it /a to
3 must want true area quit rely room move dove love
4 sale must take here list hall want mark head take
5 In ancient times persons counted on their fingers.
6 Real speedy computers and calculators do formulas.
7 Does the military use a large number of computers?
8 The missile guidance system is computer-based now.
9 Most department stores use computers for checkout.
10 Robots controlled by a computer will do hard jobs.
11 At 8:26 p.m. the word-processing material was due.
12 Did Ed Smit install the new disk drive on 7/22/96?
□□□□1□□□□2□□□□3□□□□4□□□□5□□□□6□□□□7□□□□8□□□□9□□□10

Learn to Create Documents

A big advantage of computer software programs is the ability to "save" a document you have created. Once saved, the document can be recalled at a later time for editing corrections or other reference purposes. In order for the computer to find the correct document saved in "memory," you must assign a file name to the document.

Naming a Document

Various software programs have different rules for assigning file names. Most have restrictions on the number of characters that can be used (usually no more than eight). Some specify that no numbers, symbols, or spaces may be used in the name. Before assigning file names, consult the user's manual for the software program you are using.

The name you assign a document should be meaningful. It should help you find the document in the future. Because of character limitations, you will often abbreviate file names. Many operators use codes to identify the type of document such as "let" for letters or "mem" for memorandums.

When using the software that accompanies this textbook, the drills and Measure Progress exercises for each lesson automatically are named and saved when you exit the lesson. For example, the file name for Lesson 6 would be LESSON6.

For composition exercises and document formatting applications, which are completed using the word processor, you must assign the file name. Follow these steps:

1. When either a composition or document formatting activity is selected within a lesson, the program automatically branches to the word processor. A screen menu similar to the following will appear.

2. If you want to start a new document, select the first choice, "New Document." When prompted for the document name, follow these guidelines:

For a composition exercise:

- Key LES for "Lesson."
- Key two digits for the lesson number.
- Key CM for "Composition."
- Key another numeral for the composition in the lesson. (For example, use "1" for the first composition.)
- An example of a complete file name is LES15CM1.

For a document formatting application:

- Key LES for "Lesson."
- Key two digits for the lesson number.
- Key DC for "Document."
- Key another numeral for the document number within the lesson. (Example: use "1" for the first document; "2" for the second, etc.)

An example of a complete file name is LES22DC1.

Saving a Document

After completing a composition exercise or a document formatting application, press ESC to indicate that you are done. The following prompt will appear in the center of the screen:

Use the Up-Arrow or Down-Arrow keys to highlight your choice and press Enter.

Follow these guidelines for making a selection.

1. Select "Resume Editing" if you want to return to the document to do more work.
2. Select "Save" to save your work and return to the word-processing screen to make another choice or continue your work. This command will add the document to the "Existing Files" list.
3. Select "Exit/Save" if you want to save completed work and you want to exit from the word processor. This choice returns you to the "Existing Files" menu. Your new document should now be listed. At this point, you may select or create another file or press ESC to go to the Main Menu.
4. Select "Exit Without Saving" if you want to exit from the word processor without saving any completed work. **CAUTION:** When you select this choice, you will lose any work completed during that lesson. Be careful! Work not saved cannot be retrieved.
5. Select "Check (show errors)" if you are doing a production exercise that the computer will grade.

Printing a Document

All documents must be saved before they can be printed. To print a saved document, bring the Main Menu to the screen. Select "Print Activities." A Printing Menu similar to the following will appear.

Lessons are listed by number under "Lessons." Composition exercises are listed by file names under the heading "Word Processor." Document formatting applications are listed by file names under the heading "Production." Use the Right-, Left-, Up-, and Down-Arrow keys to highlight the document you want to print and press Enter. The following prompt will appear in the center of the screen.

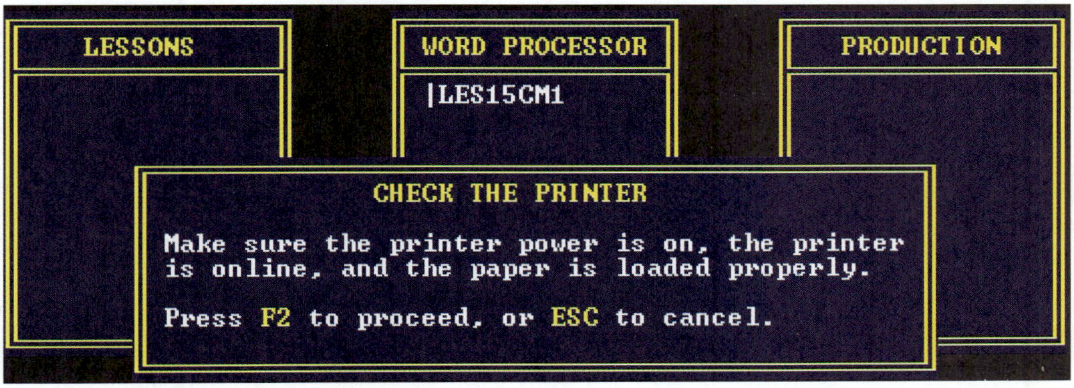

Your completed copy will include your name, the date that the document was printed, and the document file name. Retain the printout for your records or submit it to your instructor for evaluation.

It is a good idea to print your documents soon after completing them. If a document file name appears on the Printing Menu, it can be edited or printed as many times as you find necessary. Once it is removed from the menu, however, it cannot be retrieved. This software program saves only the last ten documents in each of the three categories.

Retrieving a File

When a composition or document formatting activity is selected, any documents already created, named, and saved appear on a menu titled "Existing Files." Use the Up-Arrow or Down-Arrow keys to highlight the file you want to work with and press Enter. That document will then come to the screen.

Measure Progress

Take two 1-minute timings.

Minimum goal: 22 wam with four or fewer errors 1.6 S.I.

Try to exceed the minimum goal.

```
     Word-processing programs are a very helpful tool in the modern office.  They save a lot of time in producing final copy for correspondence and different kinds of manuscripts.  Used with various types of graphics software, many very attractive report formats can be produced.  There are a number of excellent word-processing programs available, but before purchasing one, be sure to try it out to see if it meets your needs.
```

1 2 3 4 5 6 7 8 9 10

Composition Exercise

Composition exercises included in this program give you an opportunity to create original documents while gaining practice using the word processor. For these exercises you will not key in material from the textbook or the screen. The contents of each document will be your own.

Name your first composition document LES15CMP.

Compose a draft sentence for each of the words listed below. Do not worry about errors for your first attempt. Try to key quickly; do not hesitate. Just get your thoughts down.

judgment   difference   quantity   assume   realize

Proofread the document on the screen. Use the editing keys to make any corrections. Save and print the exercise.

Proofread the printout and mark any errors you may have missed. Retrieve the document to the screen and make any more corrections that may be necessary. Save and print your corrected copy.

End-of-Lesson Procedure

At the end of each lesson, you will have the following options:

1. To restart the same lesson, press the F1 function key.
2. To return to the Lessons Menu, press ESC. This action automatically will save the completed lesson.
3. To proceed to the next, or any other lesson, highlight your choice on the menu and press Enter.
4. To return to the Main Menu, press ESC again.
5. To print the lesson, select Print Activities.
6. To exit the program:
   a. Select the Exit option and press Enter.
   b. When the DOS prompt appears on the screen, remove your data disk.
   c. Turn off the monitor. (Your instructor also may ask you to turn off the computer and printer.)

16

Skill Building

GOALS

- Reinforce Previous Learning
- Increase Keying Speed
- Improve Skill in Keying Top-row Numbers
- Practice Composition Skills

Remember the "Get Ready" checklist.

REVIEW

Key each line two times.

```
1 Janice created 9,684 prizes for Tex and the queen.
2 Computers do dumb duties better than 1,000 people.
3 The number 99 is thought to be unlucky by the mob.
4 The series contained 1, 2, 3, 4, 5, 6, 7, and 189.
5 The tax yield qualified all budget annual reviews.
```

DEVELOP KEYING SKILLS WITH NUMBERS

Key across the columns.

Read four-digit numbers in groups of two: 2896 twenty-eight/ninety-six.

Key the exercise twice. Press the space bar twice between each group of numbers.

```
1 2896  3429  2338  2897  3510  2652
2 6247  2489  7898  0128  1987  3178
3 3629  1050  4264  7246  1440  4254
4 4289  2244  1312  6950  1610  1234
5 6215  6381  1510  1794  1763  0987
```

Increase Keying Speed

Only speed is analyzed and reported.

Read and key in phrases.

1 do no /my by /go at /am it /to go /go to /in an end
2 go to by my /of it at /is it in /do in go /go at it
3 her day /put the /did not /you are /new car /so any
4 rain cook boys mind pear faze tear vote fades have
5 fork pair melt hair form soak down wisp pale gowns

□□□□1□□□□2□□□□3□□□□4□□□□5□□□□6□□□□7□□□□8□□□□9□□□10

Improve Keying Accuracy

Both speed and accuracy are analyzed and reported.

Try to maintain speed, but key with control—no more than one error per line.

1 John sold 46,734 sets of pens, and Sue sold 6,472.
2 Bring 282 envelopes, 71 cards, and 36 paper clips.
3 The combination is 6 right, 2 left, and back to 0.
4 The combinations of 100 and 500 equaled 1,572,689.
5 If I add 139,462 to 157,382 will it equal 996,884?
6 Take the 32.46 from Juan and give Bettie 4,650.50.
7 My number is 749-6843. Is your number 34231-5689?
8 If number 75689 rings, transfer it to extension 4.
9 What is the total of 981, 472, 301, 695, and 4031?
10 Bring me number 462, 793, 502, 103, 986, and 6381.

Measure Progress

Exercise 1

Minimum goal: 23 wam with three or fewer errors 1.6 S.I.

Performance goals for the lesson are based on the 1-minute timings.

Take two 1-minute timings.

```
     The ability to store basic paragraphs and form letters allows great variety and the ability to individualize correspondence.  The added features of format changes, typestyle changes, and spelling checks are most attractive to various users.  A variety of word-processing programs are available. Each brand has different features that you must learn.  Some are easier to learn than others. DisplayWrite and WordPerfect are examples of two popular brands of word-processing software.  Both are excellent word-processing programs.
```

1 2 3 4 5 6 7 8 9 10

Exercise 2

Minimum goal: 20 wam with six or fewer errors

Take two 2-minute timings on the preceding paragraph.

Composition Exercise

Using the word processor, name a document LES16CM1. Key your responses to the following questions on the screen. Do not worry about format or errors for now. Just try to get your thoughts down.

1. Where do you live? (Street, city, state, zip)
2. What are your parents' full names?
3. How long have you been learning to keyboard, and who is your instructor?
4. What do you like best about learning to keyboard?
5. What were three of the most difficult things for you to learn?
6. How will you use your new keyboarding skills?

Proofread the document on the screen. Use the editing keys to make corrections. Save and print the document.

Proofread the printout and mark any errors you may have missed. Make corrections if necessary. Save and print your corrected copy.

Follow the proper end-of-lesson procedure.

17

Apostrophe, Quotation Mark, Exclamation Point, and Dollar Sign Keys

GOALS

- Reinforce Previous Learning
- Learn New Keys ', ", !, and $
- Increase Keying Speed

REVIEW

Remember the "Get Ready" checklist.

Key each line two times.

1 Computer keyboarding is a skill that creates jobs.

2 Persons who can promptly access a computer are OK.

3 If it is in the red car, you may drive it to work.

4 Now is the time to learn to use keyboarding skill.

5 Can you add 1, 2, 3, 4, 5, 6, 7, 8, 9, 10, 20, 30?

LOCATE THE APOSTROPHE " ' KEY

The ' (apostrophe) is located to the right of the ; and is keyed with the ; finger. Key this line.

;'; ;'; ;'; ;';

PRACTICE THE APOSTROPHE "' KEY REACH

Key each line two times.

Do not space before the apostrophe. Space after an apostrophe only if it is at the end of a word.

1 ;'; ;'; ;'; I'll try to find Tim's old blue coats.
2 Did you visit the children's new red brick school?
3 He bought the shirt for a week's pay. Is it Al's?
4 We'll match the companies' earnings sometime soon.
5 Ask Mr. Jones' secretary for a copy of the report.

LOCATE THE QUOTATION MARK "' KEY

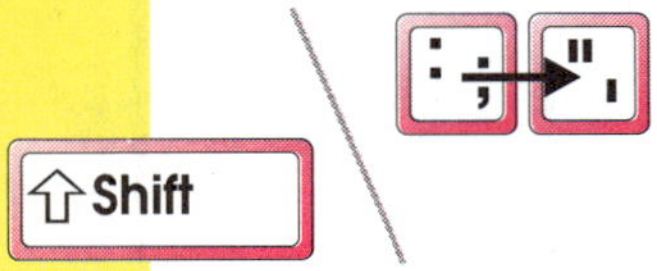

The " (quotation mark) is the shift of the apostrophe. Use the Left Shift key and the ; finger.

Periods and commas are placed inside quotation marks. The question mark is placed inside the quotation mark when it is part of the quoted material. Place the question mark outside the quotation mark when the question is not part of the quoted material.

PRACTICE THE QUOTATION MARK "' KEY REACH

Note how the question mark is used with the quotation marks in line 3.

1 ;"; ;"; ;"; Joe said, "See the newly fallen snow."
2 "I am going skiing in the mountains," said LeAnne.
3 Did you read the article, "Word Processing Today"?
4 Quen said, "I'll bring Xiu's computer home today."
5 "I have completed my class report," said Jonathan.

LOCATE THE EXCLAMATION POINT !1 KEY

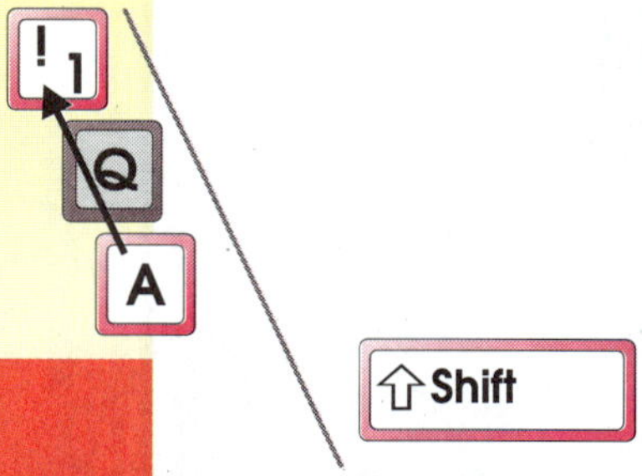

The ! (exclamation point) is the shift of the 1 and is keyed with the A finger.

a!a a!a a!a a!a

Space twice after an exclamation point at the end of a sentence.

The exclamation point is placed inside the quotation mark when it is part of the quoted material.

PRACTICE THE EXCLAMATION POINT ! 1 KEY REACH

Key each line two times.

Key and space quickly.

1 He yelled, "Fire!" Wow! Our team won the trophy!
2 Study today! Earn tomorrow! Be a success always!
3 Stop! The car is still moving! Yes! Now! Stop!
4 I hate to study on Saturdays! Help! Here! Stop!
5 That school's new principal is a real "go-getter"!

LOCATE THE DOLLAR SIGN $ 4 KEY

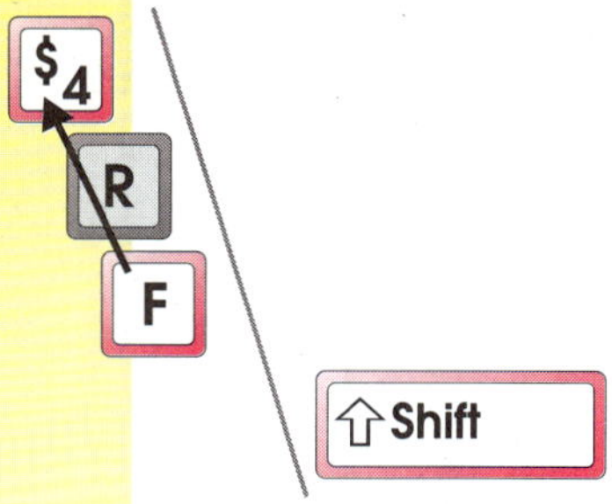

The $ (dollar sign) is the shift of the 4 and is keyed with the F finger.

f$f f$f f$f f$f

PRACTICE THE DOLLAR SIGN $ 4 KEY REACH

Key each line two times.

1 f$f $15 $380 $79 $36 $48 $4 $45.50 $374.89 $42 $89
2 Please send me $400. He owed me $12, $10, $15.50.
3 $1,234.50 The items cost $23.24, $54.28, and $300.
4 Do you have $15, $35.89, $46.21, $37.89, $4567.69?
5 The tickets were a real bargain at $20 and $50 ea.

Increase Keying Speed

Try to beat the computer and increase your speed.

Only speed is analyzed and recorded.

```
1  of it at up am me us an do of at us he if as no it
2  one way par run pad set new let vie gas has her it
3  hear trees make pain shut down hear card drab cars
4  as it is a /at my by /go to do /to no by /it is at
5  You may pay your dues when the reply form is sent.
6  A vote is the way to show what rules they desired.
7  The drills do not exercise the fingers adequately.
8  The sentences contain the letters on the keyboard.
9  Many programs are simple and others quite complex.
10 Programs that check spelling are helpful to learn.
   □□□□1□□□□2□□□□3□□□□4□□□□5□□□□6□□□□7□□□□8□□□□9□□□10
```

Improve Keying Accuracy

Now key each line above for control; no more than one error. Try to maintain your previous speed.

Measure Progress

Exercise 1

Minimum goal: 24 wam with three or fewer errors 1.6 S.I.

Performance goals for the lesson are based on the 1-minute timings.

Take two 1-minute timings.

```
     Computer literacy means having a basic
understanding of how to access and use a computer
system.  This also implies that a person has a simple
vocabulary of computer terminology. In the near
future, persons who do not have basic computer
literacy will be at a disadvantage in their home and
work lives.
     Computers in the home will keep budgets,
checking accounts, menus, and schedules of future
events.  These functions will help people to become
better organized and manage their resources more
efficiently.
□□□□1□□□□2□□□□3□□□□4□□□□5□□□□6□□□□7□□□□8□□□□9□□□10
```

Minimum goal: 21 wam with six or fewer errors

EXERCISE 2

Take two 2-minute timings on the preceding paragraphs.

END-OF-LESSON PROCEDURE

At the end of each lesson, you will have the following options:

1. To restart the same lesson, press the F1 function key.
2. To return to the Lessons Menu, press ESC. This action automatically will save the completed lesson.
3. To proceed to the next, or any other lesson, highlight your choice on the menu and press Enter.
4. To return to the Main Menu, press ESC again.
5. To print the lesson, select Print Activities.
6. To exit the program:
   a. Select the Exit option and press Enter.
   b. When the DOS prompt appears on the screen, remove your data disk.
   c. Turn off the monitor. (Your instructor also may ask you to turn off the computer and printer.)

18

Parentheses, Ampersand, and Percent Keys

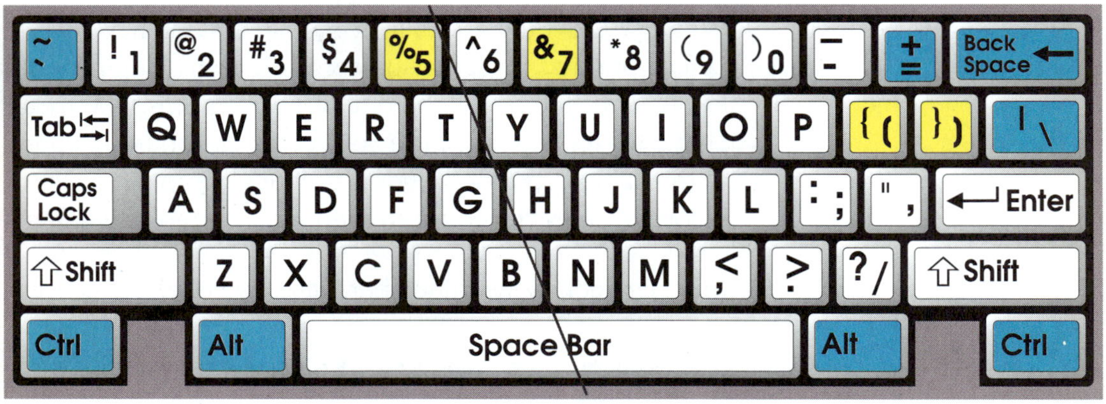

GOALS

- Reinforce Previous Learning
- Learn New Keys ( ), &, and %
- Increase Keying Speed

Remember the "Get Ready" checklist.

REVIEW

Key each line two times.

Remember the rules about punctuation and quotation marks.

```
1 Take the credenza back to Joe and let him keep it.
2 When Zoro comes home, tell him to wash the dishes.
3 The accounts are due and payable on the first day.
4 Jimmy's dad said, "Send $5.10 as soon as you can!"
5 Will said, "I'll need $4 before the trip is over!"
6 When the dog ran away, she yelled, "Stop the car!"
```

LOCATE THE LEFT PARENTHESIS (9 KEY

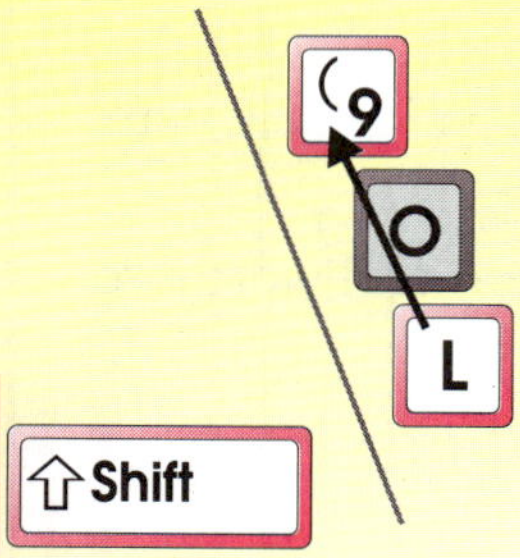

The ((left parenthesis) is the shift of the 9 and is keyed with the L finger.

```
l(l l(l l(l l(l
```

PRACTICE THE LEFT PARENTHESIS (9 KEY REACH

Key each line two times.

1(1 1(1 1(9 1(9 1(91 (40 (50 (191 (92 (10 (345

LOCATE THE RIGHT PARENTHESIS)0 KEY

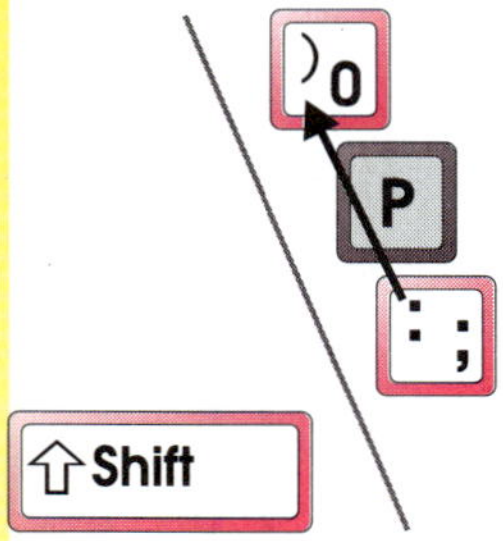

The) (right parenthesis) is the shift of the 0 and is keyed with the ; finger.

;); ;); ;); ;);

PRACTICE THE RIGHT PARENTHESIS)0 KEY REACH

Key each line two times.

;); ;); ;)0 ;)0 0) 00) 90) 10) 11) 49) 50) 21) 27)

Two spaces after :
No space after)
One space after (

PRACTICE THE LEFT AND RIGHT PARENTHESIS (9)0 KEY REACHES

1 Route these: (1) letter, (2) card, and (3) lists.
2 We will determine (a) what, (b) why, and (c) when.
3 Kenneth may (1) telephone, (2) meet, and (3) test.

Locate the Ampersand &7 Key

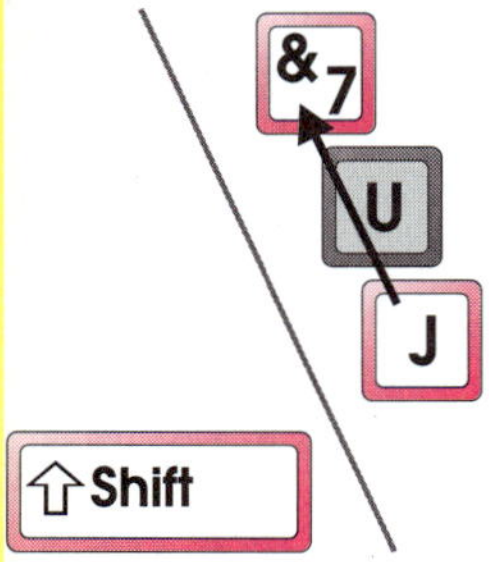

The & (ampersand) is the shift of the 7 and is keyed with the J finger.

j&j j&j j&j j&j

Practice the Ampersand &7 Key Reach

The ampersand is not used in formal writing.

Key each line two times.

1 j&j J7j j& John & Bill; Pam & Paul; Sherry & Andy.

2 George & Juao & Gail & Hua played tennis & soccer.

3 Harris & Henley & Jackson will buy all that stock.

4 Joyner & Lowenstein will merge with Chez & Varner.

5 Chan & Son and Su & Ling will move to 12 N. 82 St.

LOCATE THE PERCENT SIGN %5 KEY

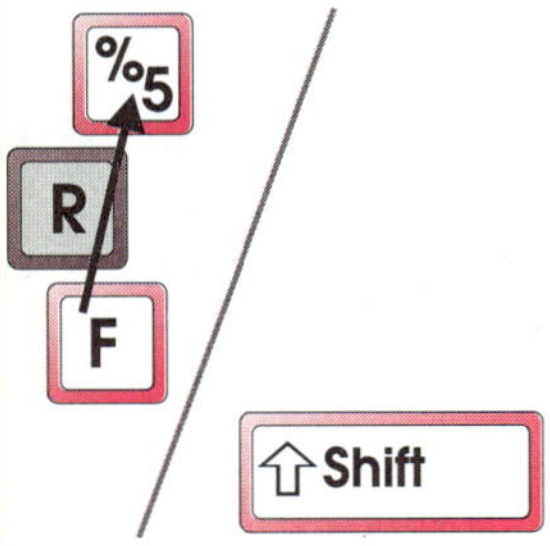

The % (percent sign) is the shift of the 5 and is keyed with the F finger.

f%f f%f f%f f%f

PRACTICE THE PERCENT SIGN %5 KEY REACH

Key each line two times.

1 f%f f%f % Please add these items: 6%, 15%, & 30%.
2 All terms are 10% discount or 15% (within 5 days).
3 Their percentage rate was 18% (we paid 15% & 12%).
4 The loan rates were 8% & 10% & 11% & 12% & 6-3/4%.
5 Discounts of 5%, 10%, 15%, 20%, and 25% are given.

INCREASE KEYING SPEED

Work to increase your speed goal.

Key each line two times for speed.

1 in go hi co to me ex he if at id or in he at in up
2 day elf may can fan did end let two sad but jar if
3 cool brat open buzz dude list mark plea good lines
4 The sale was fair; the cost was not over the mark.
5 or it at /go to do an /of an at /it is a /to no am
6 Keep your fingers on correct keys for quick speed.
7 Laser printers are fast and have printing options.
8 Many expensive laser printers make fancy graphics.
9 Desktop publishing involves multifaceted software.
10 Thermal transfer printers are economical but slow.

1 2 3 4 5 6 7 8 9 10

Improve Keying Accuracy

Now key each line on the preceding page for control. Try to maintain your speed while keying no more than one error per line. Repeat a line if you have more than one error.

Measure Progress

Exercise 1

Minimum goal: 25 wam with three or fewer errors 1.6 S.I.

Try to exceed the minimum goal.

Take two 1-minute timings.

```
     An exercise program is often used as a treatment
for muscle strain.  Proper muscle tone can improve
posture and help prevent the risk of muscle strain.
It is essential that you consult with your physician
prior to attempting any strenuous exercises.
     Exercise regularly throughout your life, and you
will feel better and stay in shape longer.  Those
persons with a regular exercise program tend to be
healthier.  Research studies have shown that people
can continue to exercise their entire lives.  They
should find an appropriate exercise for their current
physical condition.
    1    2    3    4    5    6    7    8    9   10
```

Exercise 2

Minimum goal: 22 wam with five or fewer errors

Take two 2-minute timings on the same paragraphs.

End-of-Lesson Procedure

At the end of each lesson, you will have the following options:

1. To restart the same lesson, press the F1 function key.
2. To return to the Lessons Menu, press ESC.
3. To proceed to the next, or any other lesson, highlight your choice on the menu.
4. To return to the Main Menu, press ESC again.
5. To print the lesson, select Print Activities.
6. To exit the program, select the Exit option and press Enter. Remove your data disk and turn off the monitor. (Your instructor also may ask you to turn off the computer and printer.)

19

Pound/Number, Equal, Plus, Asterisk, and At Symbols

GOALS

- Reinforce Previous Learning
- Learn New Keys #, =, +, *, and @
- Increase Keying Speed
- Improve Keying Accuracy

Remember the "Get Ready" checklist.

REVIEW

Key each line two times.

1 The usual (20% & 10%) profit margins will be used.
2 Katie said, "The discount rate is 10% on $125.50."
3 Over 58% (234) of the class voted the 4-year plan.
4 The 9-3/4% note ($13,248.25) was paid February 21.
5 ZIP codes speed the mail to everyone for February.
6 An excited red dog bit the small quiet calico cat.
7 Tex created six quaint prizes for Janice and Bill.

LOCATE THE NUMBER OR POUND SIGN #3 KEY

Remember to use proper technique.

The # (number or pound sign) is the shift of the 3 and is keyed with the D finger. When it is keyed in front of a number, it stands for number. When it is keyed after a number, it stands for pounds.

```
d#d d#d d#d d#d
```

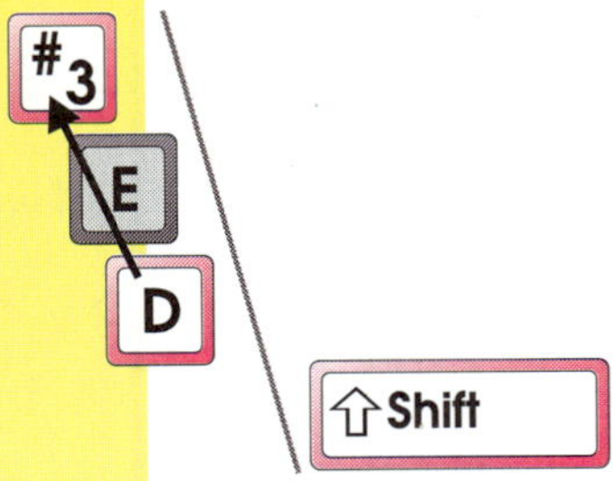

Practice the Number or Pound Sign #3 Key Reach

Key each line two times.

```
1 d#d d#d d#d 33# #29 21# #4 Will needs a #3 pencil.
2 The order calls for #4, #402, #56, #4765, & #4678.
3 Please send me items #223, #4625, #3570, & #89654.
4 Do the machines weigh 34#, 478#, 89#, 76# or 856#?
5 Orders #1459, #2370, #1498, & #1621 were for 978#.
```

Locate the Equal Sign += Key

The = (equal sign) is located to the right of the - and is keyed with the ; finger.

```
;=; ;=; ;=; ;=;
```

Practice the Equal Sign += Key Reach

Key this line two times.

```
;=; ;=; ;=; ;=; A=B G=AB 1=f 100=a 44=BC ;=;
```

Locate the Plus Sign + = Key

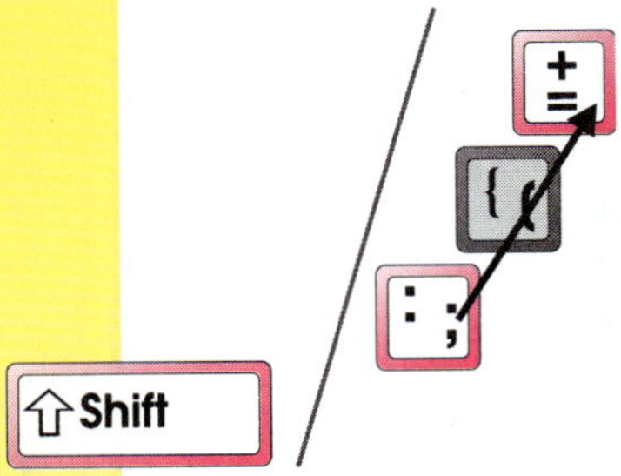

The + (plus sign) is the shift of the = and is keyed with the ; finger.

```
;+;  ;+;  ;+;  ;+;
```

Practice the Plus Sign + = Key Reach

Key each line two times.

```
1 ;+;  ;+;  ;+;  A + B + C + D = K + J  1 + 4 + 3 + 2 = 10
2 L + J + T + A = R  6 + 8 + 14 + 12 = 40  1 + 2 + 3 = 6
```

Locate the Asterisk * 8 Key

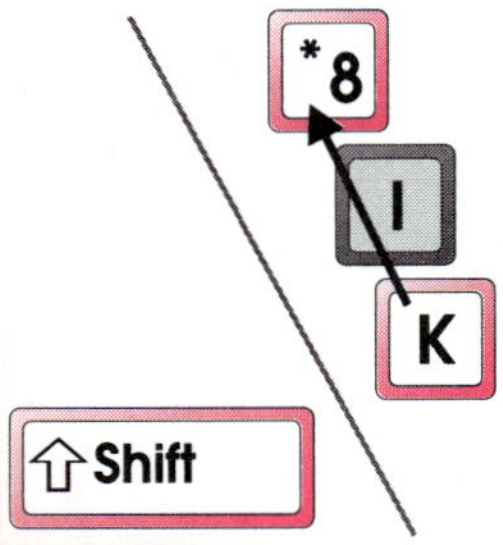

The * (asterisk) is the shift of the 8 and is keyed with the K finger.

```
k* k  k* k  k* k  k* k
```

PRACTICE THE ASTERISK *8 KEY REACH

Key each line two times.

Keep your eyes on the copy.

1 k*k k*k k*k Please see the quotation* noted below.
2 Zavier and Alexander* called for #150, #80, & #96.
3 Fill the order* with 1,287#, 345#, 789# & 27,520#.
4 Please identify the following: 16*, 18*, and 29*.
5 What is this balance* 17 + 49 + 38 = 38 + 49 + 17?

LOCATE THE AT SIGN @2 KEY

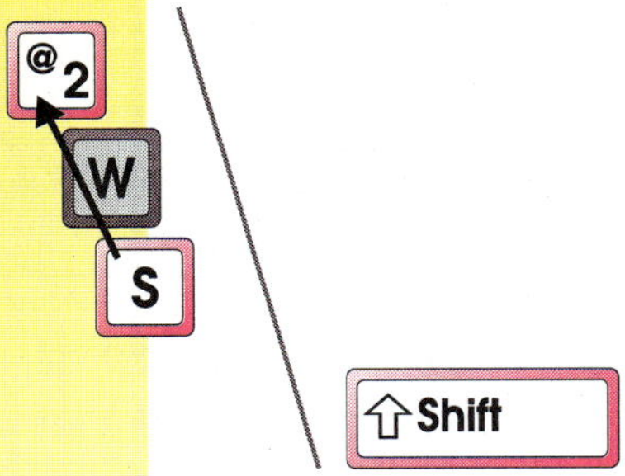

The @ (at sign) is the shift of the 2 and is keyed with the S finger.

s@s s@s s@s s@s

PRACTICE THE AT SIGN @2 KEY REACH

Key each line two times.

1 We bought #10's @ $85, #25's @ $40, & #30's @ $49.
2 The order* was for 6# @ $79, 30# @ $5, & 4# @ 20#.
3 The quotation* was 24 @ $69, 32 @ $17 & 45 @ $356.
4 The stock purchase was 10 @ $6, 20 @ $9, 35 @ $78.
5 Order 100 shares @ 59 1/8 and 200 shares @ 15 3/4.

Increase Keying Speed

Key each of the following lines two times for speed.

1 your very sent daze lead pave lose weed days time
2 near fade plea foot case took both walk hand girl
3 past due/home town/rain falls/star gaze/what then
4 Voice-input computers are being researched today.
5 In the future, voice input may replace keyboards.
6 Experts want a computer to accept various voices.
7 Tone and pitch differences make the task complex.
8 Automatic speech recognition is very complicated.
9 Acoustical ambiguity of speech may be understood.
10 For now, we must accept the faults of the system.

1 2 3 4 5 6 7 8 9 10

Try to reach a new speed goal. Beat the computer.

Improve Keying Accuracy

Both speed and accuracy are analyzed and reported.

1 Eliza purchased topaz jewelry from the quiet lady.
2 Zoe was having a quiet meal with Joyce and Bettie.
3 Jody hid the blue topaz in the vault in zone four.
4 That jigsaw puzzle caused great anxiety to Fawzia.
5 Those ballet dancers were quite nimble and lively.

Try to maintain speed, but key for control—no more than one error per line. Repeat any line with more than one error.

Measure Progress

Exercise 1

Minimum goal: 25 wam with three or fewer errors 1.8 S.I.

Try to exceed the minimum goal.

Take two 1-minute timings.

Many times software designed for one brand of computer will not run on another brand of computer. If two different brands of computers will run the same software, they are considered compatible. Incompatible computers will not run the same software programs due to differences in the disk operating systems and other internal operating systems.

Many programs are written in BASIC programming language and others use machine language. Different computers interpret the commands and languages in different ways, thus producing incompatibility.

1 2 3 4 5 6 7 8 9 10

Exercise 2

Minimum goal: 23 wam with five or fewer errors.

Take two 2-minute timings on the preceding paragraphs.

End-of-Lesson Procedure

At the end of each lesson, you will have the following options:

1. To restart the same lesson, press the F1 function key.
2. To return to the Lessons Menu, press ESC. This action automatically will save the completed lesson.
3. To proceed to the next, or any other lesson, highlight your choice on the menu and press Enter.
4. To return to the Main Menu, press ESC again.
5. To print the lesson, select Print Activities.
6. To exit the program:
   a. Select the Exit option and press Enter.
   b. When the DOS prompt appears on the screen, remove your data disk.
   c. Turn off the monitor. (Your instructor also may ask you to turn off the computer and printer.)

20 Remaining Symbols

GOALS

- Reinforce Previous Learning
- Learn Other Symbols
- Learn to Center and Underline Text

Remember the "Get Ready" checklist.

Review

Key each line two times.

1 Two #3 or four #6 pencils @ $.50 ea. will = $9.00!
2 Invoice #4876 was paid by checks #248, #763, #215.
3 The formula for the spreadsheet is (A7 + B3 = C8).
4 The quote* was for 150 @ $14, 275 @ $63, 86 @ $94.
5 The prize elm was cut down by five angry citizens.
6 A quaint bronze box held four green emerald rings.
7 You can learn to keyboard easily with zero errors.

Learn Other Symbols

The locations of certain symbols will vary on different microcomputer keyboards. Study the keyboard on your machine to determine the location of any additional symbols.

Practice Other Symbols

Practice keying these lines two times each. Omit the lines containing any symbols not on your keyboard.

1 This ^ sign means 4^4 or four to the fourth power.
2 Is A > B or J > L or K > M or Q < P or Y < Z or X?
3 Is [AA - BB] = [KK - LL] or [MM + ZZ] = [JJ + RR]?
4 You can load the WordPerfect program with WP51\WP.

Increase Keying Speed

Try to set a new speed goal.

Key each of the following two times for speed.

1 Both mail norm hand shot half gain loss bare dues
2 zone bone home star tear each when bull over then
3 for it /for a /and the /but all /had she /and all
4 all of the /for you /you are /she was /I will see
5 Voice output from a computer is fairly primitive.
6 Linking a phone and computer enhances capability.
7 Video conferencing reduces business travel costs.
8 Communications can be made better with computers.
9 Many computer voices sound very mechanical to us.
10 Soon letters will be replaced by electronic mail.
□□□□1□□□□2□□□□3□□□□4□□□□5□□□□6□□□□7□□□□8□□□□9□□□10

Improve Keying Accuracy

Try to maintain speed, but key with control—no more than one error per line. Repeat any line with more than one error.

Both speed and accuracy are analyzed and reported.

1 Roma's letter indicated that he could type 50 wam.
2 Jo said, "Call the operator--the tape has broken!"
3 Create a new subdirectory for \memos for the file.
4 Johnson, Smith & Co.* mailed the order on 12/6/97.
5 The desk is 6' wide and 42" high--a bargain @ $98.
6 The invoice she typed was for 6 #2 loads @ $10 ea.
7 We will need 48 @ $145.98 to place the next order.
8 Order 12 #2 pens & 36 #6 (hard) pencils @ $.20 ea.
9 Sarah knew that (1/2 + 1/4) - (2-1/4 - 1-1/2) = 0.
10 Profits were 110% last quarter and for last month.

Learn Automatic Horizontal Centering

Most microcomputer word-processing software programs have an automatic centering feature. This feature is activated by entering an automatic centering command when keying the line to be centered. Some programs use one of the function (F) keys to enter this command; others use the CTRL plus an alphabetic key, such as CTRL+C or CTRL+X. In this program, the F6 key is a toggle switch that controls centering. Follow these steps to activate the automatic centering feature:

1. Centering can be done only on a word-processing screen.
2. Press the F6 key. Centering is now activated.
3. Key the text you would like to have centered. If you want more the one line of text centered, you can press Enter and then key the next line.
4. Press the F6 key to turn off the centering feature.

Practice Centering

Reminder: F6 is the automatic centering key.

Using the word processor, name a document LES20DC1. Center the following lines using the automatic centering feature. Remember: The F6 key is a toggle switch, which means that you only need to turn it on once to center all of these lines. Press Enter at the end of each line.

```
      MICROCOMPUTER FORMATTING
        Automatic Centering
      Word-Processing Programs
Keyboarding with Technique and Skill
```

Print the document. Study the printout to see if each line is centered properly. Proofread and mark any errors you may have missed. Make corrections if necessary. Save and print your corrected copy. When satisfied with your work, have the computer check your document. Press ESC and select the check option.

Learn to Underline

Reminder: F8 is the key to underline copy.

Underlining on a microcomputer usually requires a special command. When using other software, consult the software manual to determine the procedures for that particular software. In this software, the F8 key is the toggle switch that controls underlining. Follow these steps to underline copy.

1. Underlining can be done only on a word-processing screen.
2. Before keying the text to be underlined, press the F8 key to start the underline. Notice that the word "Underline" appears on the prompt line.
3. Key the text. The text to be underlined appears highlighted on the screen.
4. Do not space at the end of the copy to be underlined. Press the F8 key to end underlining.

Practice Underlining

Name a document LES20DC2. Practice these sentences. Use the F8 key to begin and end underlining.

1 Not all software uses the same procedures to underline.

2 Consult the software manual to determine the procedures for underlining.

3 Her book, Introduction to Office Automation, was well received.

4 Have you read the book The Stock Market Report?

5 John's book, A Beginner's Guide to Wise Decision Making, was a best-seller.

Print the document. Proofread and mark any errors you may have missed. Make corrections if necessary. Save and print your corrected copy. When satisfied with your work, have the computer check your document. Press ESC and select the check option.

Measure Progress

Exercise 1

Minimum goal: 25 wam with two or fewer errors 1.6 S.I.

Try to exceed the minimum goal.

Take two 1-minute timings.

```
     Soon people will be able to talk to their
computers.  These new computers will allow all types
of creative work.  Think of interacting with a
talking word-processing program as you prepare a
letter or report.  People who use these computers
will require a new type of thinking skill.  They will
have to learn to arrange their thoughts in a logical
order.
    1    2    3    4    5    6    7    8    9   10
```

Minimum goal: 23 wam with four or fewer errors
1.4 S.I.

Exercise 2

Take two 2-minute timings.

```
     A compound word is made from two or more words combined to form a new word.  A compound word may be written as one word, as two or more separate words, or as a hyphenated word.  Regardless of how it is formed, each newly formed word is considered one word.  In order to figure out the meaning, consider the separate meaning of each word and then combine them to arrive at a new definition.  The new definition will contain meaning from both of the combined words.
```

1 2 3 4 5 6 7 8 9 10

Composition Exercise

Using the word processor, name a document LES20CM1. Briefly think about a job you have had, currently have, or would like to have in the future.

1. Make a list of the words that describe the characteristics of the job. Center each word using the F6 key.
2. Write four or five sentences using these words to describe the position. Using the F8 key, underline the words in your sentences that come from your original list.
3. Do not worry about errors on your first attempt. When finished, proofread the document on the screen. Use the editing keys to make any corrections.
4. Save and print the document. Proofread the hard copy and mark any errors you may have missed. Retrieve the document and make corrections as necessary. Save and print your corrected copy.

End-of-Lesson Procedure

At the end of each lesson, you will have the following options:

1. To restart the same lesson, press the F1 function key.
2. To return to the Lessons Menu, press ESC.
3. To proceed to another lesson, highlight your choice and press Enter.
4. To return to the Main Menu, press ESC again.
5. To print the lesson, select Print Activities.
6. To exit the program, select Exit option.

21 Skill Building

GOALS

- Reinforce Previous Learning
- Increase Keying Speed
- Improve Keying Skills

Remember the "Get Ready" checklist.

Review

Key each line two times.

```
1 Zelda earned extra pay for a violin she gave Quin.
2 Jeff asked Kim to explain the zoo project to Jack.
3 All you need do is practice to refine your skills.
4 Key as quickly as you can, and you will be expert!
5 Ken said, "I'll meet you at the park at 4:30 p.m."
6 The stock market quote* was for 100 shares @ $975.
```

Increase Keying Speed

Only speed is analyzed and reported.

```
1 who was it/was the boy/call the man/all of it/will he/ask me
2 for hers/the men/one of them/was the/are you/and the/was all
3 can she/let the/tore past fast/they play hard/they must lead
4 both half shot/mark zone lines/turn each over/must mark down
5 send cash now/sale must take/here list hall/want marked sale
6 Personal computers have lost popularity because of software.
7 All workers should field-test software before use in office.
8 Sharing terminals has expanded the use of computer networks.
9 Lengthy keyboarding projects are best done by trained staff.
10 Several word-processing software packages are on the market.
```

11 Consider how long it takes to learn a program before buying.
12 Unfortunately, many programs do not deliver what's promised.
13 Notebook computers help people do work away from the office.
14 Managers use computers to prepare reports while on the road.

    1   2   3   4   5   6   7   8   9   10   11   12

Improve Keying Accuracy

Both accuracy and speed are analyzed and reported.

1 An average annual income for an adult is actually amortized.
2 Behold the bonus buys brought back the best bountiful books.
3 Catch the crazy cat quickly! Carry the calf to that corral.
4 Deep diving does drive dumb ducks daffy. Diets deny donuts.
5 Easy earnings earn early debts. Easy exit earns in the end.
6 Five fervent firefighters find funds in foundation benefits.
7 Great Golden Gate grant got good publicity for the governor.
8 Hair is hard to have. Harvey heaved that herring head high.
9 Igor intends to initiate the initial initiative immediately.
10 Jill just junked Joe's jalopy. Jana jabbed the juicy jewel.
11 Kim knew the kettle was a keepsake. Know how to knit kites.
12 Labor is like leisure if you laugh at your load. Let loose.
13 Mega machines mean the maximum mastery of major measurement.
14 Neither Nels nor Nate neglected to negate Ned's nominations.
15 Oxen obstruct the only overpass. You owe the order the oil.
16 Provoke payees to pay promptly. Partial payments permitted.
17 Quan equipped the quartz quarry with quietly quality quotas.
18 Rest and relaxation render diverse rewards for the recruits.
19 Sam's seven system symbols are sequenced in successive sets.
20 Theory throws time travel to tomorrow. Tentative trial set.
21 Ursula was unsure about your uproar. Usurp universal unity.
22 Vain VIPs value victory. Value of a good valve was evident.
23 Workers wish Winona would waste less wild water in workouts.

24 Xenophobics exhibit extreme anxiety of Xingu's xenolith sea.
25 Yearly yields for young yams yoyo in the Yucatan and Yanzee.
26 Zigzagged zoning mazes crazed zany, zingy, zippy zoologists.

Measure Progress

Exercise 1

Minimum goal: 25 wam with two or fewer errors 1.4 S.I.

Take two 1-minute timings.

The model 1150 printer is very fast and produces letter-quality print. The 5015 dot matrix printer produces excellent graphics.

Turnaround time is the amount of time from the keying of data to the printing out of the results. The turnaround time on the last job was about 15 minutes.

1 2 3 4 5 6 7 8 9 10

Exercise 2

Minimum goal: 23 wam with four or fewer errors 1.7 S.I.

Try to maintain speed, but key with control.

Take two 2-minute timings.

Sometime in the future you may need to make a decision to stay with a company or move on to new challenges. This type of decision causes a great amount of stress. When you are under stress, you usually do not make good decisions.

A career change requires a thorough study of the alternatives and the effects of each. Making important decisions takes time; therefore, one should not make career decisions on a crisis basis. Consider the alternatives and weigh the pros and cons of each. Reach important decisions in a rational way, and you will be pleased with the decision.

1 2 3 4 5 6 7 8 9 10

EXERCISE 3

Minimum goal: 20 wam with six or fewer errors 1.5 S.I.

Take two 3-minute timings.

Entering data into a computer system can be accomplished in a number of ways. You can input data from a soft or hard disk. The keyboard can be used to type in alphabetic and numeric data. Light pens can be used to touch or draw on the computer screen.

Graphics also can be entered using a graphics tablet directly attached to the central processing unit. In the future, many computers will have voice input, which will allow the user to have conversations with the computer and merely tell the computer what to do.

Advanced computer designs are creating computers that can learn and do their own problem solving. You will be able to teach the computer unique things that you want done a certain way, and then the computer will solve a given program using the data you have entered with the method you have taught it.

1 2 3 4 5 6 7 8 9 10

COMPOSITION EXERCISE

Name a document LES21CM1 in the word processor. Compose a short paragraph (four or five sentences) describing how you would respond to the following problem.

Problem: You are assigned to a team to complete a project. Two people on the team are not doing their share of the work. This affects what you and the other team members are responsible for doing. What steps you can take to solve the problem?

When finished, proofread the document on the screen. Use the editing keys to make any corrections. Save and print the document.

Proofread the printout and mark any errors you may have missed. Retrieve the document and make corrections as necessary. Save and print your corrected copy.

Follow the appropriate end-of-lesson procedure.

UNIT 3-
NUMERIC KEYPAD

22

Learn the Numeric Keypad 4, 5, 6, 7, 8, and 9

GOALS

- Reinforce Previous Learning
- Learn 4, 5, 6, 7, 8, and 9 Using Numeric Keypad
- Learn to Enter Numbers in Column Format

Remember the "Get Ready" checklist.

REVIEW

Key each line two times.

```
1 Sometimes a fine argument can obtain good success.
2 Roz was excited about eating a quiet meal with Bo.
3 The winning number for a quaint gift was fourteen.
4 How many computers were ordered with topaz chairs?
5 The police officer yelled, "Stop that yellow car!"
6 Please call me at 748-6972 (extension 15) at 8:30.
```

LEARN THE NUMERIC TEN-KEY KEYPAD

Most microcomputers have a numeric keypad that is used for material containing intensive numeric applications. Numeric data can be entered faster with the ten-key keypad than with the top-row number keys.

On the IBM PC, the numeric keypad is located to the right of the alphabetic keyboard. This location may differ on other microcomputers, but the arrangement of the numeric keys is basically the same. The ten-key keypad arrangement is the same as on electronic calculators.

To activate the numeric keypad, press the Num Lock key. On some keyboards, this key is located above the numeric keypad. On other keyboards, it is located below the numeric keypad. After the data has been entered, press the Num Lock key again to resume regular keyboarding functions. This key is a toggle switch.

The Principles of Reading Numbers

The same principles of reading numbers that apply to top-row numbers also apply to the numeric keypad. Review Lesson 13 before beginning the next section.

Locate the 4, 5, and 6 Keys

Use proper technique.

The home keys on the numeric keypad are the 4, 5, and 6. Place the J K L fingers on the 4, 5, 6 keys.

Assume Correct Finger Position

When operating the numeric keypad, use the correct finger position:

1. Rest your fingers lightly over the home keys.
2. Keep your fingers curved and upright.
3. Use quick, snappy strokes.

The ten-key keypad is most often used to key numbers or amounts that appear in columns. To keep the numbers in column format, strike Enter after keying each line of the column. On most microcomputers, the Enter key is located to the right of the 3 key. Use the little finger of the right hand (the ; finger) to quickly strike Enter after keying a group of numbers. On some microcomputers, the Enter key is located to the left of the 4 key. In this case, use the 4 finger to strike the Enter key.

Practice the 4, 5, and 6 Key Reaches

Look at your fingers as you make the initial reaches. Then practice keying these drills until you can key them by touch. Key down each column.

You do not need to total these columns.

1	4 4	5 5	4 4	4 4 4	4 4 4	4 4 4	4 4 4	5 5 5
2	4 4	5 4	5 5	5 5 5	5 5 5	5 5 5	5 5 5	4 4 4
3	4 4	4 4	6 6	6 6 6	6 6 6	6 6 6	6 6 6	6 5 5
4	5 5	4 5	6 4	6 4 6	6 5 4	4 5 6	6 5 4	6 5 4
5	5 5	4 4	6 5	6 5 4	4 5 6	6 5 4	5 4 6	5 4 5
6	5 5	5 5	4 6	4 5 6	4 6 6	4 5 5	6 5 5	6 4 5
7	6 6	6 6	5 6	5 6 6	5 4 4	6 4 4	5 4 4	5 4 6
8	6 6	6 5	6 4	4 5 6	4 5 6	4 5 6	4 6 5	5 4 6
9	6 6	5 6	6 5	6 5 4	6 5 4	6 4 5	6 5 4	5 5 6
10	5 5	6 5	4 5	5 4 6	4 6 6	5 4 5	6 5 5	5 4 4

Locate the 7, 8, and 9 Keys

The 7, 8, and 9 keys are located in the row above the 4, 5, and 6 keys. Keep your fingers resting on the 4, 5, and 6 keys and practice the reach to the 7, 8, and 9 keys.

Keep your fingers curved and strike each key quickly.

Practice the 7 Home, 8 ↑, and 9 Pg Up Key Reaches

Look at your fingers as you make the initial reaches. Then practice keying these drills until you can key them by touch. Key down each column.

1	44	444	55	555	66	666
2	47	777	58	888	69	999
3	77	776	88	857	99	695
4	44	475	55	846	66	599
5	77	577	88	648	96	498
6	74	745	85	548	69	897
7	47	547	58	488	99	579
8	77	647	88	748	66	789
9	44	747	55	857	96	878
10	47	574	58	784	69	945

Practice All Numeric Keypad Key Reaches

Practice keying these drills until you can key them by touch. Key down each column.

1	946	495	987	976	478	878	4798
2	857	699	458	675	794	699	6457
3	748	978	864	598	556	556	8596
4	956	846	758	467	678	787	7845
5	465	759	846	745	875	645	5968
6	546	469	987	698	989	575	7546
7	759	546	746	748	677	849	8495
8	864	648	847	659	985	658	5678

Measure Progress

Exercise 1

Minimum goal: 25 wam with two or fewer errors 1.3 S.I.

Try to exceed the minimum goal.

Take two 1-minute timings.

Software quality is often not as good as we would prefer. Many programs have flaws or bugs in them. Your best bet is to try out the software before buying it or be sure the company has a return policy. If software is to be used in a classroom setting, it should be tried out by students before it is purchased. Classroom software needs to be dependable.

1 2 3 4 5 6 7 8 9 10

Exercise 2

Minimum goal: 23 wan with four or fewer errors 1.7 S.I.

Take two 2-minute timings.

Debugging a program means to remove the flaws to get the program to perform properly. The term "debug" comes from the past when computers had a large number of electromagnetic relays. The heat generated by the relays attracted bugs and lint, so debugging actually meant removing the bugs from the relays.

Computers are becoming smaller and smaller as advances in chip technology are made. The ability to build very small and compact computers will allow great advances in robotics and artificial intelligence.

1 2 3 4 5 6 7 8 9 10

Minimum goal: 20 wam with six or fewer errors 1.6 S.I.

Try to exceed the minimum goal.

Exercise 3

Take two 3-minute timings.

Artificial intelligence implies that the computer will be able to learn and change its behavior based on new information. The computer's behavior will become adaptive. The user or owner of a robot will be able to teach it special or required behavior designed to accomplish a given task.

Imagine being able to teach your personal robot to cook, clean house, tend the garden, or be a security guard at night. How about teaching it to take care of your pet? In reality, the possibilities are limited only by the imagination of the owner.

The possibilities for the use of artificial intelligence in business are unlimited also. Programmers of these expert systems may be called knowledge engineers. The careers available in this field are very exciting.

1 2 3 4 5 6 7 8 9 10

Composition Exercise

Using the word processor, name a document LES22CMP. Compose a short paragraph (four or five sentences) describing how you would respond to the following problem. Do not worry about errors on your first attempt.

Problem: A new student at your school asks how to apply for admission and register for a course. List, in order, the steps that the student should follow.

When finished, proofread the document on the screen. Use the editing keys to make any corrections. Save and print the document. Proofread the hard copy and mark any errors you may have missed. Retrieve the document and make corrections as necessary. Save and print your corrected copy.

Follow the appropriate end-of-lesson procedure.

23

Learn the Numeric Keypad 1, 2, 3, 0, and Decimal Point

GOALS

- Reinforce Previous Learning
- Learn 1, 2, 3, 0, and . Using the Numeric Keypad

Remember the "Get Ready" checklist.

EVIEW

Key each line two times.

```
1 Good skills are crucial in information processing.
2 Queries to the computer prompted a quick response.
3 Some people are initially afraid to use computers.
4 Programs that do not operate properly are not fun.
5 The measurement for the living room was 12' x 26'.
6 Call 1-800-893-4952 for information about records.
```

LOCATE THE 1 End, 2 ↓, AND 3 Pg Dn KEYS

The 1, 2, and 3 keys are located in the row below the 4, 5, and 6 keys. With your fingers resting on the 4, 5, and 6 keys, practice the drills until you can key them by touch.

Practice the 1 End, 2 ↓, and 3 Pg Dn Key Reaches

Key down the columns.

1	44	444	55	555	66	631
2	11	111	22	222	33	321
3	41	144	52	257	63	723
4	14	511	25	722	36	123
5	44	614	55	521	66	443
6	11	751	22	124	33	322
7	41	681	25	219	63	113
8	14	171	52	812	36	324
9	11	145	22	176	33	321
10	14	164	25	152	63	362

Remember to read the numbers in groups.

Practice All Numeric Keypad Key Reaches

Key down the columns.

1	111	456	324	478	641	721	4251
2	222	123	586	581	986	423	6382
3	333	789	732	692	321	647	4793
4	453	983	346	736	158	313	6821
5	936	458	329	137	326	892	5147
6	123	312	831	462	215	476	9284
7	322	241	762	151	163	298	2673
8	243	156	363	231	224	214	3461
9	641	752	143	591	642	519	2572

LOCATE THE 0 Ins AND . Del KEYS

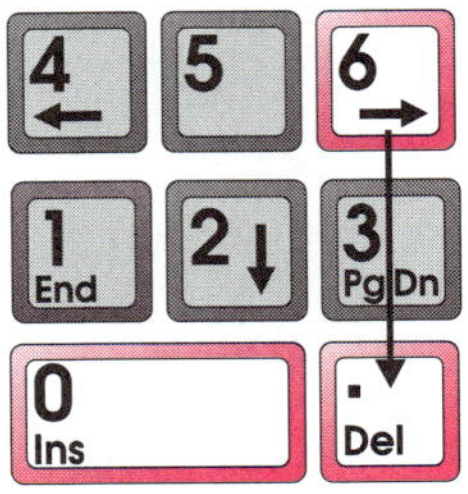

The location of these keys may vary on different keyboards. Use the appropriate finger for the location of the keys on your keyboard.

PRACTICE THE 0 Ins AND . Del KEY REACHES

The 0 is keyed with the thumb (on most machines). The . (decimal) is keyed with the 6 finger (on most machines). Practice keying these drills until you can key them by touch. Key down the columns.

The decimal points do not need to align in this exercise.

1	44	410	666	4.50	45.90
2	11	203	.66	0.5	6.150
3	00	120	6.6	.01	72.49
4	40	010	44.3	.60	6.381
5	10	050	2.01	5.0	00.01
6	04	400	3.56	60.	49.04
7	40	700	45.3	.01	63.01
8	01	303	65.9	.05	78.02
9	00	101	98.7	.11	63.73
10	07	809	41.5	6.80	89.40

Practice All Numeric-Keypad Key Reaches

Practice keying these drills until you can key them by touch. Remember to apply the number-reading principles to these drills. Key down the columns.

.005	54.12	231.1	7801	1234	10987
6.05	20123	45.12	6420	5678	21098
.212	1.001	11.33	6947	9009	32109
22.6	.0005	104.0	4279	8765	43210
2.14	1.789	20.10	8346	4321	54321
1.03	.6112	100.1	1059	0246	65432
.001	761.2	20.10	2001	8135	76543
70.0	40.03	233.9	3042	7901	87654
61.1	987.1	87.06	4110	3690	10987
34.5	492.6	05.01	6710	4905	23947

Measure Progress

Exercise 1

Minimum goal: 25 wam with one or fewer errors 1.7 S.I.

Try to exceed the minimum goal.

Take two 1-minute timings.

Legal secretaries, medical records secretaries, and general office secretaries must learn keyboarding skills. A good typist only needs to learn the special computer keys to make the transition from typist to computer keyboarder. It is not difficult to become proficient on a computer keyboard if you are a good typist. The arrangement of the keys is essentially the same.

1 2 3 4 5 6 7 8 9 10

EXERCISE 2

Minimum goal: 23 wam with three or fewer errors 1.6 S.I.

Take two 2-minute timings.

File cabinets may become totally obsolete when the paperless office is fully implemented. All records will be electronically stored on various media. Think of the trees that will be saved.

When voice recognition is perfected, keyboarding also may become obsolete. All one will have to do is give a verbal command, and the computer will respond. Using this computer will require a new skill of talking composition.

□□□□1□□□□2□□□□3□□□□4□□□□5□□□□6□□□□7□□□□8□□□□9□□□10

EXERCISE 3

Minimum goal: 20 wam with five or fewer errors 1.6 S.I.

Try to exceed the minimum goal.

Take two 3-minute timings.

The main purpose in keyboarding skill is to efficiently enter data for the computer to process. If the data is entered incorrectly, then the output will contain errors. This idea is expressed by the phrase "Garbage in, garbage out." Keyboarding speed is essential; however, accuracy is also important. Usually one works on speed and then concentrates on correctness. In the final result, both speed and accuracy are essential.

At this point in your keyboarding program, you should be proficient in keying alpha and numeric information. You should be able to use correct techniques and to key by touch. Your speed should be increasing, and you should be improving your accuracy also.

□□□□1□□□□2□□□□3□□□□4□□□□5□□□□6□□□□7□□□□8□□□□9□□□10

Composition Exercise

Using the word processor, name the document LES23CM1. Suppose that you are very good at keyboarding, and your supervisor at work decides that you can answer some of the company correspondence. Using the word processor, compose a short paragraph (four or five sentences) describing how you would respond to the following problem. Do not worry about errors on your first attempt.

Problem: An irate customer has written a letter complaining about a repair person who made an appointment but never showed up.

When finished, proofread the document on the screen. Use the editing keys to make any corrections. Save and print the document.

Proofread the printout and mark any errors you may have missed. Retrieve the document and make corrections as necessary. Save and print your corrected copy.

End-of-Lesson Procedure

At the end of each lesson, you will have the following options:

1. To restart the same lesson, press the F1 function key.
2. To return to the Lessons Menu, press ESC. This action automatically will save the completed lesson.
3. To proceed to the next, or any other lesson, highlight your choice on the menu and press Enter.
4. To return to the Main Menu, press ESC again.
5. To print the lesson, select Print Activities.
6. To exit the program:
   a. Select the Exit option and press Enter.
   b. When the DOS prompt appears on the screen, remove your data disk.
   c. Turn off the monitor. (Your instructor also may ask you to turn off the computer and printer.)

UNIT 4-
FORMATTING

24 Skill Building and Formatting Reports

GOALS

- Reinforce Previous Learning
- Increase Keying Speed
- Improve Keying Accuracy
- Learn to Double-Space
- Learn to Format Unbound Reports

Remember the "Get Ready" checklist.

REVIEW

Key each line two times.

1 The zoo contained a number of very quaint animals.
2 Compare words a minute (wam) scores to gain speed.
3 Warm up fast! Use all fingers! Relax the muscle!
4 Their overhead for the first quarter will be >10%.
5 Jane said, "Stop the tape! We produced 10% @ $1."
6 My number is 804-763-1529; Jack's is 203-723-7651.

INCREASE KEYING SPEED

Key each line two times.

1 her day/put the/did not/you are/new car/any one/take the car
2 make the mail list/turn left here/roll past the mark/call it
3 must want true area quit rely room move dove love sale minds
4 sale must take here list hall want mark head take note fifth
5 town star send sale fees fast cold half gain must tell reply
6 Everyone needs to know keyboarding within the next ten years.
7 Spreadsheets are used to prepare account ledgers and budgets.
8 Many software packages have tutorials and on-line assistance.
9 Paperless offices and modems initiate new cottage industries.
10 People working at home will eliminate many city traffic jams.
11 Menu-driven software lists accessible options for procedures.
12 A spreadsheet program lets me easily execute math operations.
13 Computers facilitate basing decisions on the up-to-date data.
14 A license agreement states how software programs can be used.

1 2 3 4 5 6 7 8 9 10 11 12

Improve Keying Accuracy

Key each of the following sentences concentrating on accuracy—no more than one error per sentence. If you do not reach the accuracy goal, repeat the sentence. Try to maintain your already achieved speed.

```
1 The tight mobs galloped at high rates until the two tripped.
2 The lower price on parking made it cheaper to drive the car.
3 Wax or tallow spilled on the wolf as he prowled the schools.
4 A zebra sped past the zany chap napping under the palm tree.
5 A lawyer verified that a violent explosion caused the quake.
6 A van was acquired to give extra transportation to the lazy.
7 It is crazy to spend vast amounts to visit the exotic lands.
8 The plumber had to quickly fix a leak to calm our anxieties.
9 Robots were used to quell the acid flow from that explosion.
10 Daily planning allows Tim to fix goals and make quick moves.
```

Measure Progress

Exercise 1

Minimum goal: 25 wam with one or fewer errors 2.0 S.I.

Try to exceed the minimum goal.

Take two 1-minute timings.

```
     Databases are collections of facts and figures
that a person or organization needs to perform
certain operations.  Examples of databases could
include names and addresses, telephone numbers, bank
balances, various accounting ledgers, paragraphs for
letter construction, and other specific data needed
by an organization.
    1    2    3    4    5    6    7    8    9   10
```

Exercise 2

Take two 2-minute timings.

Minimum goal: 23 wam with three or fewer errors 1.4 S.I.

Your speed is slowly improving. Very soon you will be keying faster than 25 words per minute. As you progress, your speed and accuracy will also increase. It is rewarding to learn a new skill. Your new skill in keyboarding will pay handsome returns for your efforts.

Persons with keyboarding skill and word-processing knowledge are in great demand. You will find it much easier to enter data into your computer now that you have a touch system of keying. The time you have spent in learning to keyboard will pay many dividends in the future.

1 2 3 4 5 6 7 8 9 10

Exercise 3

Take two 3-minute timings.

Minimum goal: 20 wam with five or fewer errors 1.6 S.I.

Try to exceed the minimum goal.

Silicon chips are the nervous system of the computer. The chips are covered with very fine pathways that form circuits. Small currents of electricity move along the pathways. Each of the circuits is designed to perform certain functions that allow the computer to execute various commands. The small pulses that race along the chip's circuits are called "bits." These bits add, subtract, compare, store, and do a variety of other tasks when the computer system is on. The circuits or designs in the chips are chemically bound onto silicon wafers.

The design of a microcomputer is amazing. The small computers of today can perform tasks that the largest computer of several years ago could not perform. What will the future hold in store in computer technology?

1 2 3 4 5 6 7 8 9 10

Learn to Double-Space

Many documents and keyboarding projects require variable spacing between each line of copy. Standard between-line spacing is usually referred to as "single-space." The most popular alternative is called "double-space." Double-spacing leaves one blank line between each keyed line of copy. Check the manual that came with the word processor you are using to learn how to double-space copy.

If you are using the software that accompanies this textbook, follow these steps to double-space copy.

1. Changing line spacing can be done only when using the word-processor portion of this program.
2. When the word-processing screen first appears, a message on the format line indicates that the default setting is "Single-Space."
3. The prompt line at the bottom of the screen indicates that the F5 function key controls spacing.
4. To change to double-spacing, press the F5 key. The format message now changes to "Double-Space."
5. All copy that you now enter will appear double-spaced on the screen and when you print copy.
6. To return to single-spaced copy, press F5 again until the format line reads "Single-Space."
7. Single-space, double-space, and triple-space are available in this word processor.

Remember: F5 is the key that controls single- and double-spacing.

Practice Line Spacing and Review Center and Underline

Using the word processor, name the document LES24DC1. Key the following announcement. Double-space the copy. Center each line of the announcement (use the F6 key). Underline the last line (use the F8 key).

```
THE DESKTOP PUBLISHING CLUB

Cordially invites you to attend

A SOFTWARE DEMONSTRATION

on

Tuesday, January 15

at 12:15 p.m.

Computer Laboratory

RSVP 555-8923 by January 10
```

Proofread the copy on the screen. Use the editing keys to make corrections. Save and print the announcement.

Proofread the printout and mark any errors you may have missed. Pay close attention to capitalization, line spacing, centering, and underlining. Retrieve the document and make corrections as necessary. When satisfied, have the computer check your work. Save and print your corrected copy.

Composition Exercise

Using the word processor, compose two short paragraphs describing how you would respond to the following problem. Do not worry about errors on your first attempt. Name the document LES24CM1.

Problem: You and another person are being considered for a promotion. The supervisor has asked each of you to write about your personal characteristics and qualities that would qualify you for the promotion. What do you write about yourself?

When finished, proofread the document on the screen. Use the editing keys to make any corrections. Save and print the document.

Proofread the printout and mark any errors you may have missed. Retrieve the document and make corrections as necessary. Save and print your corrected copy.

Learn to Format Unbound Reports

A report is a written summary of an activity or a presentation of data and information concerning a specified topic. Reports are designed to communicate, in a concise format, the results of various activities such as projects, meetings, assignments, and research.

Reports may be classified as informal or formal. The informal report is often used in business to present factual information. Formal reports are used to present the results of a study or investigation and are usually presented in bound format.

Look at the sample one-page unbound report format on page 142. This report follows one acceptable format. Formats for reports vary depending on the style manual you are using. Always consult the appropriate manual before keying a report.

Follow these steps to layout a one-page informal report.

1. Leave a 2-inch top margin. Key the title centered and in all capital letters. Remember that the software automatically leaves a one-inch top margin, so press Enter until the cursor is on line 13 (two inches).
2. Turn on double-spacing.
3. Key the body of the report.

4. Indent each paragraph five spaces (to the first default tab).
5. Use the 1-inch default side margins and the 1-inch default margins for the bottom of the page.
6. Use automatic word wrap. Do not strike Enter at the end of each line. Strike Enter to end a paragraph.

Formatting Exercise

1. Using the word processor, name a document LES24DC2. Key the model unbound report on the next page using the layout directions you just learned.
2. Proofread your copy on the screen. Use the editing keys to make corrections. Save and print the document.
3. Compare your printed copy with the model. Mark any errors you missed. Save and print your corrected copy. Have the computer check your document when you are satisfied with your work.

End-of-Lesson Procedure

At the end of each lesson, you will have the following options:

1. To restart the same lesson, press the F1 function key.
2. To return to the Lessons Menu, press ESC. This action automatically will save the completed lesson.
3. To proceed to the next, or any other lesson, highlight your choice on the menu and press Enter.
4. To return to the Main Menu, press ESC again.
5. To print the lesson, select Print Activities.
6. To exit the program:
   a. Select the Exit option and press Enter.
   b. When the DOS prompt appears on the screen, remove your data disk.
   c. Turn off the monitor. (Your instructor also may ask you to turn off the computer and printer.)

2"

GREAT BRITAIN ← centered

England, Northern Ireland, Scotland, and Wales make up the United Kingdom of Great Britain and Northern Ireland. These four countries, under one government, are located in Northwestern Europe. Most people refer to the country as Great Britain, Britain, or the United Kingdom.

1" → The capital of Britain is London. English is the official language. The country is governed by a Prime Minister and Parliament. Great Britain is inhabited by about one percent of the world's total population and has few natural resources; yet it has been one of the world's most important countries. ← 1"

The British are credited with starting the Industrial Revolution. The revolution, which began in the 1700s, started in the cotton textile industry and later spread to other areas such as mining and transportation. The revolution evolved as machines gradually replaced hand labor, and factory systems were developed. For instance, people used to work at home spinning cotton into yarn and weaving yarn into material.

The Industrial Revolution made Britain one of the world's richest manufacturers and the world's greatest traders. During the eighteenth century, the British Empire began to crumble. There were then the two world wars and a series of economic crises. Today, the United Kingdom is no longer a leading world power. They have lost the huge empire and economic strength.

1"

25 Skill Building and Formatting Business Letters

GOALS

- Reinforce Previous Learning
- Increase Keying Speed
- Improve Keying Accuracy
- Learn to Format Personal Business Letters

Remember the "Get Ready" checklist.

Review

Key each line two times.

1 She quickly learned the skills of the zany clowns.
2 That quiet zoologist studies a variety of animals.
3 Get the new file! Hold the copy! Send a receipt!
4 Take a break! Go home early! Catch those horses!
5 The order was 2 doz. #3's $ $.02 ea. and 4 @ $.05.
6 This order should create >10% profit or >15% loss.
7 Marty said, "Dial this number, 706-483-9251, now!"

Increase Keying Speed

Key each line two times.

1 of at or in an it if is to te ti do id di my fa go ho lo got
2 how cut big put hot ten lie was per its eve cab dot cub spot
3 jars sale rain give fair its yours mine hers his ours theirs
4 use the/let her/off the/end the/was for/was he/did he/get it
5 head home now/dues paid count/very open sites/come home soon
6 send reply quick/took noon lunch/play her hunch/give a bunch
7 I cover the computer keyboard. Keying skill takes practice.
8 Quick fingers are a result of proper practice and technique.
9 Electronic mail lets you correspond with a lot of coworkers.
10 Use of an outline saves time when writing a business report.
11 Spreadsheets help people compute and diagnose business data.

1 2 3 4 5 6 7 8 9 10 11 12

Improve Keying Accuracy

Key each of the following sentences concentrating on accuracy—no more than one error per sentence. If you do not reach the accuracy goal, repeat the sentence. Try to maintain your already achieved speed.

1 Mules were used for moving heavy dirt and plowing the field.
2 People wish to avoid dieting but decide not to give up food.
3 World golfers wallow in sorrow when missing short tee shots.
4 It is sad that exact spending quotas sparked a palace panic.
5 A zoo was not the best place to exhibit the valued elephant.
6 A lazy eagle soared over the majestic mountains and valleys.
7 Jet planes quickly break through foggy skies across borders.
8 Be sure that workers have exact ways to zero in on problems.
9 Get good results, which may amaze me, when you view options.
10 Simulated ivory is now used on pianos to save the elephants.

Measure Progress

Exercise 1

Minimum goal: 25 wam with one or fewer errors 1.8 S.I.

Try to exceed the minimum goal.

Take two 1-minute timings.

Computer-assisted instruction is when the computer actually performs teaching functions. The computer may present lessons, provide drill and practice, conduct assessment, and assign future lessons based on current skill levels. Good computer-assisted instruction requires student interaction and will adapt to the student's needs for enrichment or remedial instruction.

1 2 3 4 5 6 7 8 9 10

Exercise 2

Take two 2-minute timings.

Minimum goal: 23 wam with three or fewer errors 1.7 S.I.

Try to exceed the minimum goal.

The central processing unit of a computer receives every instruction coming into the computer system and sends out all resulting messages. It processes all operations of the system. It controls all functions and stores various commands and operating programs. Some central processing units can perform computations and operations faster than a millionth of a second. The central processing unit is thought of as the brains of the computer.

Optical disk memory systems are now available. They have a greatly increased memory capacity. In the future, their storage capacity is expected to double. This will produce cost and space saving.

1 2 3 4 5 6 7 8 9 10

Exercise 3

Take two 3-minute timings.

Minimum goal: 20 wam with four or fewer errors 1.7 S.I.

Try to exceed the minimum goal.

The cathode ray tube is a large vacuum tube. Images are produced on the front of the tube by tiny charges of electricity hitting the phosphor on the screen, causing it to glow in the shape of letters, numbers, or graphics that you have keyed. These screens come in various sizes.

Each microcomputer brand has some different special function keys. Most are very similar, and the alphabetic keys are usually alike, as well as the numeric keypad. Your major task will be to learn the function keys for the various software packages. Each word-processing program is different. The differences, however, are not very great once you have mastered the basic word-processing concepts.

1 2 3 4 5 6 7 8 9 10

Composition Exercise

Using the word processor, name a document LES25CM1. Compose a short report describing how you would respond to the following problem. Do not worry about errors on your first attempt.

Problem: You work in an office that needs to copy a great number of correspondence, invoices, and sales reports. However, your office area does not have a copy machine—you must use a copier located on another floor. Compose a draft of a short one-page report justifying the purchase of a copier for your department.

When finished, proofread the document on the screen. Use the editing keys to make any corrections. Save and print the document.

Proofread the printout and mark any errors you may have missed. Retrieve the document and make corrections as necessary. Save and print your corrected copy.

Learn to Format Personal Business Letters in Block Style

Refer to the example on page 148.

Study the personal business letter on page 148. Look carefully at the formatting directions and how the document is arranged on the page. Then read the following information for formatting and punctuation guidelines.

Block style is an efficient letter style because all lines begin at the left margin. The letter should be centered on the page, leaving approximately equal space at the top and bottom and in the left and right margins. When using automated equipment to key letters, the default margins are used by most operators. Proper placement of the letter is achieved by varying the space between some of the parts of the letter; for example, between the dateline and the inside address.

A note about punctuation: There are two punctuation styles commonly used in today's business world—standard and open. In **standard punctuation**, a colon follows the salutation and a comma follows the complimentary close. In **open punctuation**, no punctuation follows either the salutation or the complimentary close. Each business decides which format to use. The formats are not combined. Use one or the other.

A personal business letter contains the following parts:

1. **Return Address.** All letters should have a return address. Sometimes the company name and return address are preprinted on the stationery, so the return address does not need to be keyed. The preprinted name and address are called a **letterhead**. Most personal business letters are keyed on plain paper; therefore, the return address is keyed above the dateline. The return address should begin approximately 2 inches from the top of the page on line 13. This space may be adjusted if needed for shorter or longer letters. Leave two spaces between the two-letter state abbreviation and the ZIP code.

2. **Dateline.** Key the dateline immediately below the return address. This line includes the month (spelled out), the day, and the year.
3. **Inside Address.** Key the inside address approximately 4 lines beneath the dateline. This space may vary, based on the length of the letter. If the letter is directed to a particular person, the inside address includes a courtesy title (such as Ms.) or professional title (such as Dr.) with the name, and the complete mailing address.
4. **Salutation.** Begin the salutation a double-space below the inside address. The salutation usually begins with "Dear," followed by the courtesy title or professional title and the addressee's last name. In standard punctuation, key a colon after the salutation. If the letter is directed to a company instead of a person, use the salutation "Ladies and Gentlemen."
5. **Body.** Begin the body of the letter a double-space below the salutation. The body is usually single-spaced, with a double-space between paragraphs.
6. **Complimentary Close.** Key the complimentary close a double-space below the body. In standard punctuation, key a comma after the complimentary close.
7. **Signature Block.** Key the name of the person writing the letter 3 lines below the complimentary close to allow space for the handwritten signature.

Formatting Exercise

1. Name a document LES25DC1. Key the model letter on page 148. Follow the format instructions above.
2. Proofread your copy on the screen. Use the editing keys to make corrections. Save and print the document.
3. Compare your printed copy with the model. Mark any uncorrected errors you may have missed. Pay attention to the spacing between parts of the letter.
4. Retrieve the document and make corrections as necessary. Save and print your corrected copy. When you are satisfied with your work, have the computer check you document. Press ESC and make the selection for checking.

2"

Return Address → 719 Cole Place
Birmingham, AL 35203

Dateline → May 22, 1995

4 blank lines (5 returns)

Inside Address → Microburst, Inc.
200 Innsbrook Place
Suite 800
San Diego, CA 92138

double-space

Salutation → Ladies and Gentlemen:

double-space

1" margin

1" margin

Body

On August 15 I purchased your new software package, "QuickType." The program disk loads properly, and the program runs. However, when I press the F1 key as indicated for "Help," the main menu appears on the screen. I have reloaded the program several times and am still unable to access the "Help" files when needed.

double-space

If you know of a solution to this problem, please send me instructions. If you do not know how to solve this problem, I would appreciate receiving a new copy of the program as my original may be defective or damaged.

double-space

Closing → Sincerely yours,

3 blank lines

Signature Block → Jason Hefler

End-of-Lesson Procedure

At the end of each lesson, you will have the following options:

1. To restart the same lesson, press the F1 function key.
2. To return to the Lessons Menu, press ESC. This action automatically will save the completed lesson.
3. To proceed to the next, or any other lesson, highlight your choice on the menu and press Enter.
4. To return to the Main Menu, press ESC again.
5. To print the lesson, select Print Activities.
6. To exit the program:
    a. Select the Exit option and press Enter.
    b. When the DOS prompt appears on the screen, remove your data disk.
    c. Turn off the monitor. (Your instructor also may ask you to turn off the computer and printer.)

26

Skill Building and Formatting Tables

GOALS

- Reinforce Previous Learning
- Increase Keying Speed
- Improve Keying Accuracy
- Learn to Set Tab Stops
- Learn to Format Simple Tables

Remember the "Get Ready" checklist.

Review

Key each line two times.

1 The judge awarded six quotas at a zoology exhibit.
2 That lazy ox caused Quincy extra anxiety and envy.
3 All reports should be clear, concise, and correct.
4 Communication skills are critical for job success.
5 I think it is time for all of us to learn a skill.
6 Ken's grades were three A's, two B's, and two C's.
7 The meeting will be held at 8:30 a.m. on March 25.

Increase Keying Speed

Key each line two times.

1 move ahead soon/take the lead/take this list/wind blows hard
2 take your time/play fair now/quit your post/found extra room
3 If you want to be good at keyboarding, set up practice time.
4 Office procedures are vital to ensure compliance with rules.
5 Offices are becoming more involved with interactive systems.
6 An advanced workstation using a 32-bit processor is popular.
7 On the job, it is necessary to work promptly and accurately.
8 Correctly designed systems interface easily with technology.
9 Software entails application programs and operating systems.
10 Types of command languages involve the use of function keys.
11 There's a large increase in computer usage by the workforce.
12 Local area networks make it possible to use electronic mail.

1 2 3 4 5 6 7 8 9 10 11 12

Improve Keying Accuracy

Both speed and accuracy are recorded.

```
1  Big brown bears barter for berries better than tiny bunnies.
2  Can credit cause cash to collapse?  Can it be a catastrophy?
3  Obnoxious odor in oceans is offensive to oysters and otters.
4  Perfect people prefer positive political posts and practice.
5  Quails are quite quick.  Conquer the quaint queasy quotient.
6  To excel Evan must exhibit extra excitement and not excuses.
7  Yummy yak yogurt and yoga yielded Yonil's youthful yearning.
8  The maze dazzled and dazed the zany, crazy, frizzy zoo gang.
9  Vacuums are vacant of various vapors.  Veto the verbal vote.
10 Wild waves washed away the wreckage.  Wan winds wailed west.
```

Learn to Set and Change Tab Settings

Note: Use the F7 key to change tab settings.

Most word processing software allows the user to set tab stops wherever they are needed. Variable tab settings are often needed when creating tables and other columnar applications. Until now, you have used only the default five-space paragraph indent tab stop. Your software does allow you to set tabs.

To set new tab stops or clear existing tab stops in this program, follow these steps:

1. Tabs may be set or cleared only at a word-processing screen.
2. At a blank word-processing screen strike F7 to display the "ruler" line near the top of the screen. The L on the ruler shows the location of the left margin. The R shows the location of the right margin. Each dot (.) indicates one space along the line and a small square appears every five spaces. A lower case t indicates any space where a tab is now set.
3. The cursor should be at the left margin. Use the Left- or Right-Arrow keys to move the cursor back and forth across the ruler line.
4. To set a new tab stop, move the cursor to the spot where you want a tab to appear. Once there, strike t. A t should now appear at that spot. A tab stop is set.
5. To remove (delete) an already set tab stop, move the cursor to an existing t. Once there, strike the DEL (delete) key. The t will be replaced with either a dot or a small square. The tab stop is cleared.
6. After setting or deleting tab stops, press Enter to start or resume a word-processing activity.

Practice Changing Tabs

Exercise 1

Using the word processor, name a document LES26DC1. First remove the default tabs. Follow the steps for setting tabs and set a tab every ten spaces from the left margin.

Space	Strike	Space	Strike	Space	Strike	Space	Strike	Space	Strike	Press
10	T	10	T	10	T	10	T	10	T	↵

Set new tab stops.

Key the following exercise. Key across the columns.

```
Kid(Tab)dim(Tab)fur(Tab)fun(Tab)guy(Tab)buy ↵
may       wet       gum       hut       pat       zip ↵
gun       quo       hut       jim       lot       fat ↵
tax       cue       red       cat       for       and ↵
```

Proofread your document on the screen and then print it. Proof the printout and mark any errors you may have missed. Make corrections if necessary. Save and print your corrected copy. When you are satisfied with your work, have the computer check your document.

Exercise 2

Now create a new document and name it LES26DC2. Clear the existing tab stops. Set the first tab at five spaces and tab stops every ten spaces after that. Key the following exercise. Key across the columns. Strike Tab before keying the first word and strike Tab after keying each word. Press Enter at the end of each line.

```
     about     could     labor     place     spent     until
     again     doubt     least     price     start     voice
     begin     drive     leave     quick     store     water
     carry     force     north     round     these     whose
     color     happy     paper     south     trust     write
```

Proofread your document on the screen and then print it. Proof the printout and mark any errors you may have missed. Make corrections if necessary. Save and print your corrected copy. When you are satisfied with your work, have the computer check your document.

MEASURE PROGRESS

EXERCISE 1

Minimum goal: 25 wam with one or fewer errors 1.3 S.I.

Take two 1-minute timings.

When you are distracted, it helps to concentrate on your copy. Some distractions can be eliminated with a little effort. When people are talking too loudly, a courteous request to talk a little quieter will usually accomplish your goal. If this does not work, you can buy a small set of soft ear plugs designed to block out noise.

1 2 3 4 5 6 7 8 9 10

EXERCISE 2

Minimum goal: 23 wam with three or fewer errors 1.4 S.I.

Try to exceed the minimum goal.

Take two 2-minute timings.

The types of pressure on the job will include time deadlines, noise, co-workers who distract you, and personal problems. Even when you are at work, things that are worrying you at home will often affect your job. It is not easy to concentrate in a distracting environment.

If you have good keyboarding skills and have mastered proper techniques and the touch method, one major source of distraction will be eliminated. The major source mentioned is having to look at the keys as you keyboard.

1 2 3 4 5 6 7 8 9 10

Exercise 3

Minimum goal: 20 wam with four or fewer errors 1.5 S.I.

Try to exceed the minimum goal.

Take two 3-minute timings.

```
     At this point in your progress, you should be able to key at least 25 words a minute without looking at the keyboard.  You should be exhibiting proper techniques and feel confident about your skills.  Your new skills will be useful in keying programs, word processing, and correspondence.
     People who have not acquired keyboarding skills will find less of a market when trying to find a job in business and industry.  Many people who are already on the job will need to learn microcomputer keyboarding.  Often change is threatening; however, in this case, it means greater efficiency and much improved copy.
     As you continue to practice and observe proper techniques, your speed and accuracy will increase, and you will feel pride in knowing that you have acquired a new and marketable professional skill.
1 2 3 4 5 6 7 8 9 10
```

Composition Exercise

Using the word processor, name a document LES26CM1. Compose two or three short paragraphs describing how you would respond to the following situation. Do not worry about errors on your first attempt.

Situation: Describe in your own words why you think keyboarding is a valuable skill for everyone.

When finished, proofread the document on the screen. Use the editing keys to make any corrections. Save and print the document. Proofread the printout and mark any errors you may have missed. Retrieve the document and make corrections as necessary. Save and print your corrected copy.

Learn to Format Simple Tables

Tables are a concise way of presenting complex data. They may range in complexity from simple two-column tables with a main heading to those with several levels of headings and many columns. Tables should be centered vertically (top to bottom) and horizontally (left to right) on the page. Tables may be presented alone on a page or incorporated into letters, reports, and memorandums.

Study the two-column table on page 157. Follow these general guidelines for formatting.

1. Center tables horizontally and vertically on the page. (If a table is to be incorporated into another document such as a letter or report, center it horizontally and leave two blank lines above and below the table.)
2. Center the main heading. Key it in all capital letters. Double-space after the title.
3. Format the body of the table in columns. The body may be single- or double-spaced, depending on the layout.
4. Center the columns horizontally, leaving a constant amount of space between each column. This space usually ranges from 4 to 8 spaces.
5. Align word columns on the left and numerical columns on the right or at the decimal point.

Determine the Vertical Center

To center text vertically on a page, determine how many blank lines to leave at the top before you begin keying. Follow these steps to center the table vertically:

1. Know the number of vertical lines available on the paper you are using. Standard 8½ by 11-inch paper has 66 vertical lines (11 inches x 6 lines per inch).
2. Determine the number of printed and blank lines in the copy to be keyed. For the table on page 157:

   Count the number of lines, including blank lines, to be keyed. In this case, the number is 15.

   Subtract the lines to be keyed from the total lines available on the page.

Available	66
Used	-15
Unused	51

   Divide the unused lines by 2 to determine the number of blank lines to leave for the top margin. Disregard any fraction. Add 1 line to the number of lines calculated and begin keying on this line.

   51 , 2 = 25½ Drop fraction: 25 + 1 = 26

   Begin keying on line 26.

3. Some microcomputer software leaves a set amount of space at the top before printing begins. Check the software you are using and include those lines as a part of your count from the top. Remember: This software automatically leaves 6 blank lines in the top margin.

Determine Horizontal Placement of Columns

You can use the automatic features of your software to simplify the horizontal centering of a table. Using the word processor, name a document LES26DC3. Follow these step-by-step directions to key the model table on page 157 using automatic features.

1. Determine the vertical center. Press Enter until you reach that line. Press the F5 key to change to double-spacing. Remember, if you have set the software for double-spacing, the cursor will move two lines each time you press Enter. On the correct line key the title and press F6 to center it. Press Enter.
2. Key the longest entry from each column. This is called the "key line." In this table, the longest lines in each column are:

   ```
   Volunteers for Literacy (8 spaces) Ms. Bettye Peoples
                                   ↑
   ```

   (Add 8 spaces for between column spacing.)
3. Notice that the line is centered because the centering key, F6, is still activated.
4. Note the position where the first column, Volunteers for Literacy, starts. It should be at position 19. Note the position where the second column, Ms. Bettye Peoples, starts. It should be at position 50.
5. Press the F7 key to bring the ruler line to the screen. Clear all existing tabs. Set a tab for column 1 at position 19 and a tab for column 2 at position 50. Press Enter to return to the document.
6. Delete the key line. Press F6 to turn off the centering.
7. Key the table. Key across the columns. Press Tab before keying the first column and then to move to the second column. Press Enter at the end of each line.
8. Proofread the document on the screen. Use the editing keys to make any corrections. Save and print a copy. Compare it with the model. If the table is not properly centered vertically and horizontally, key it again making adjustments as necessary. Save and print your corrected copy. When you are satisfied with your work, have the computer check your document.

Follow the appropriate end-of-lesson procedures.

Line 26 →

PROGRAM ADVISORY COMMITTEE

double-space

Literacy Foundation	Dr. Ed Jones
Volunteers for Literacy	Mr. John Smith
United Way, Inc.	Ms. Bettye Peoples
State Literacy Director	Dr. Lynn James
Governor's Office	Ms. Joyce Booth
Ford Foundation	Dr. Milton Hirsh
State University	Dr. Paul Simeon

↑ 8 spaces

↑ Position 18

↑ Position 49

Appendix A
Computer Keyboarding Glossary

The following terms are used throughout this textbook and in most word processing and computer application books.

alphanumeric Letters of the alphabet, numbers, and/or symbols used to refer to the keyboard, as in alphanumeric keys.

arrow A key on some computers that you use to move the cursor or to delete something you have keyed. Arrows move the cursor backward, forward, up, or down.

author The person who writes a document.

backspace A key on some computers that moves the cursor back one space to the left and deletes keyed characters at the same time.

BASIC Beginner's All-Purpose Symbolic Instruction Code. A popular language for micro- and minicomputers.

binary Consisting of two parts. In mathematics, the binary system has two numbers: 0 and 1.

bit Binary digit of either 0 or 1. The smallest unit that computers read. In computer programs, most bits are arranged in groups of eight to represent letters, numbers, or symbols.

boot To load all the instructions that your computer needs to start and run a specific program.

break On many computer keyboards, a key that will stop the action of a program or process.

bug A mistake or error in a computer program or in the design of a computer.

byte A string of eight bits that stands for a letter, number, or symbol.

cancel In word processing, a key that is designated to stop a previous command or instruction.

catalog A command to the computer to list all the files stored in a software source.

character A symbol, letter, or number on the keyboard.

command An order that the computer processes.

control key (CTRL) A key that interrupts a computing process. It usually is keyed with another key.

copy In word processing, a key or process that will move data from one location to another.

cursor A small line or square that appears on the screen to indicate where the next keystroke will appear. The cursor can be moved around the screen with the arrow keys.

data The information, numbers, letters, and symbols that you input into the computer for processing.

data processing The work the computer does to input material into a specific program.

delete In word processing, a key that tells the computer to remove data that has been input.

Enter The key that sends a message from the keyboard to the central processing unit. Also, in word processing, after keying a line of text, pressing Enter will return the cursor to the beginning of the next line. On some keyboards, Return and Enter have the same functions.

file A set of records that is stored under a specific name or label.

graphics The artwork, diagrams, pictures, charts, and graphs that are displayed on the screen or by the printer.

hard copy The paper copy of information stored in a computer or a document.

hardware All parts of the computer system except the software program. Hardware includes the CPU, the keyboard, the monitor, and the printer.

indent In word processing, a key or combination of designated keys that temporarily moves the left-hand margin of a screen or page.

input Adding data into the computer. Can be done from the keyboard or from a disk.

keyboard The input device for word processing. It has the alphanumeric, symbol, and function keys.

memory The area in a computer in which data is stored for processing.

output The data displayed, printed, or stored as the result of a specified process.

printer The computer hardware that makes printed pages from data.

software The programs and instructions that run the computer and allow the user to perform different functions.

store To hold data on a disk in memory or on a tape for future use.

turnaround time The amount of time from the input of data to the output or completion of the job.

word processing An automated system or procedure that provides for correspondence and composition functions.

word wrap A feature of most word-processing programs that moves a word that will not fit within the right margin to the beginning of the next line.

Appendix B
Optional Computer Applications Lessons

Key these exercises using the word processor.

Learn Data Entry

Many software programs provide a series of prompts and menus that require the operator to enter data. The operator must then make responses to these prompts and enter them in the spaces provided. The following Learning Activities will simulate different types of data entry operations.

Learning Activity 1

Key the answers to the following simulated prompts. Begin each response at the left margin. Double-space between each entry. Print a copy of the responses.

```
1. Enter today's date.
2. Enter your name and social security number.
3. Enter your current address.
4. When did you start this course? ____ ____ ____
                                    MO   DA   YR
5. How would you describe your current keyboarding
ability?
6. How will you use your new keyboarding skills?
7. List the first and last names of five friends and their
approximate ages.  Start names at the left margin; for
ages, set a tab 25 spaces from the left margin.
8. List and number sequentially ten qualifications you
feel you have for a future job.
```

Learning Activity 2

1. Key the following addresses. Use the OCR envelope style. Double-space between entries. Do not key the column headings. Set the following tabs:

```
Employee No.    15
Name    20
Address    38
ZIP    60
```

(So that the numbers in column 1 will align on the right side, space in one time before keying the first nine numbers.)

2. Print a copy of the exercise.

Employee No.	Name	Address	ZIP
1	SMITH J MR	147 EAST BLVD	
		RENO NV	89525-4832
2	JENKINS R MS	519 BAKER ST	
		ELMIRA NY	14932-9842
3	O'MALLEY J DR	SUITE 7 92 PARKWAY	
		ALBUQUERQUE NM	87102-3394
4	HARRISON B MS	5916 BROAD CT	
		RICHMOND VE	23261-4039
5	SHERIDAN L MR	ROUTE 2 BOX 47	
		KNOXVILLE TN	37916-9834
6	PETERS J DR	ROUTE 1 BOX 598	
		ABERDEEN SD	57401-8928
7	BROCK S MS	4219 SOUTH PLACE	
		BOZEMAN MT	59715-4921
8	BORAX N MR	10 PARK PLACE	
		NEW YORK NY	10121-3929
9	WILLIAMS B MR	123 PINE ROAD	
		OREM UT	84057-1229
10	LOVELL A MS	14876 PLAZA CIRCLE	
		LEBANON PA	17042-9876
11	REGESTER A MS	527 CHARLES RD	
		GREENVILLE SC	29611-2394
12	HALL L DR	19 LONG PINE ROAD	
		BURLINGTON NC	27215-9843
13	WEIS J MS	ROUTE 98 BOX 24A	
		CHARLESTON WV	25319-0293
14	FOISE B MS	5917 GREY RUN	
		CALGARY AB	
		CANADA	J8M 4T2
15	MEESE R DR	17 KNOTT PLACE	
		ST JOHNS NF	
		CANADA	9S 4R6
16	SMOTHERS L MR	59 HILLTOP	
		DURANGO CO	81301-8943

17	ZENO R MS	ROUTE 5 BOX 2	
		SAN JUAN PR	00911-9832
18	HARROD Z MR	58972 BULL RUN	
		ST ALBANS VT	05478-9821
19	CLEMONS T DR	APT 7 INNSBROOK	
		SEATTLE WA	98143-9832
20	DOWNS P MR	OUTPOST 6	
		FAIRBANKS AK	85621-9432

Learn Computer Applications

In order for a computer to perform specified functions, it must have a program to run. Programs are written in various languages. The central processing unit of a computer understands machine language which is numerical (binary). Since it is most difficult to write programs in a code of unique number combinations, languages were created that use words and other symbols to construct programs. Commonly used high-level programming languages include the following:

BASIC (Beginner's All-Purpose Symbolic Instruction Code)
COBOL (Common Business-Oriented Language)
FORTRAN (Formula Translator)
PL I (Programming Language I)
ALGOL (Algorithmic Language)
RPG (Report Program Generator)
Pascal (Named after Blaise Pascal)
C (Child of B Language)

Often, a programmer creates programs at the keyboard. At other times, the programmer writes them out and someone else may enter them at the keyboard. Most programs have to be edited many times. This requires hard copy and reentry of the changed program using the keyboard.

Format a BASIC Program

In order to acquaint you with the various languages and to further develop your keyboarding skills, several programs are presented in different languages for you to enter at the keyboard. The first program is written in BASIC, which is a popular programming language for writing instructions or programs for the microcomputer.

Learning Activity 3

1. Key the following excerpt from a BASIC program. Proof your copy carefully to be sure that every space, punctuation mark, and character is correct. Any error could cause the program to run improperly.

2. Begin the numbers at the left margin. Begin the text five spaces from the margin at the first tab.
3. Print a copy and compare it with the model. Mark any uncorrected errors on the printout.

```
10  HOME: PRINT "PRACTICE"
20  PRINT "COPYRIGHT (C)"
30  PRINT "IBM-PC"
40  PRINT
45  PRINT "THIS PROGRAM ALLOWS YOU TO KEEP"
50  PRINT "STOCK RECORDS"
60  PRINT "YOU CAN LIST ALL OF YOUR STOCKS"
100 PRINT "GAIN OR LOSS, AND THE"
210 PRINT "TOTAL IN YOUR PORTFOLIO."
220 GOSUB 410
230 IF CP = 5 THEN CM = 225
240 IF CP = 3 THEN CM = 18
250 IF CP = 1 THEN CM = 6
270 IF CP <1 OR CP >5 THEN 190
280 PRINT
290 PRINT "ENTER THE REQUIRED AMOUNT"
300 INPUT P
320 PRINT "ENTER THE INTEREST RATE (%)"
330 INPUT X
340 PRINT
350 ON CP GOTO 400
360 FOR T = 1 TO 10
370 NEXT T
380 RETURN
390 REM DAILY INTEREST
400 HOME
410 PRINT "WEEK # ";N;" : STOCK PRICE=$";BA
420 GOSUB 459
440 PRINT :GOSUB 580
450 PRINT "DO YOU WISH A PLOT?"
460 PRINT "1-YES 0-NO"
470 INPUT T
480 IF A = 1 THEN 370
490 END
```

FORMAT A COBOL PROGRAM

COBOL is a popular language for business applications software. The line identifying labels have been omitted from the following program. The computer usually adds these automatically in a COBOL program.

LEARNING ACTIVITY 4

1. Key the following excerpt from a COBOL program. Proof your copy carefully to be sure that every space, punctuation mark, and character is correct. Any error could cause the program to run improperly.
2. To format a COBOL program, begin at the left margin and set tabs every four spaces.
3. Print a copy and compare it with the model. Mark any uncorrected errors on the printout.

```
IDENTIFICATION DIVISION.
PROGRAM-ID. PRACTICE COBOL.
AUTHOR. UNKNOWN.
ENVIRONMENT DIVISION.
INPUT-OUTPUT CONTROL.
FILE CONTROL.
    SELECT INFD ASSIGN TO READER.
    SELECT BOOK-FILE ASSIGN TO DISK.
    SELECT SORT-FILE ASSIGN TO SORT DISK.
    SELECT PRINT ASSIGN TO PRINTER.
DATA DIVISION.
FILE SECTION.
FD INFD
    DATA RECORD IN INPUT-RECORD.
01 INPUT-RECORD.
    02 CALL-NUMBER-IR.
    02 AUTHOR-IR.
    02 TITLE-IR.
    02 DATE-IR.
    02 ITEM-NUMBER-IR.
    02 PRICE-IR.
    02 DISCARD-CODE-IR.
FD BOOK FILE
    DATA RECORD IS BOOK-RECORD.
2030-BUILD-EXIT.
    EXIT.
```

```
3000-REPORT SECTION.
3010-REPORT-CONTROL.
    PERFORM 3020-INITIALIZATION.
    PERFORM 3030-REPORT-BODY.
    GOTO 3040-REPORT-TERMINATION.
3020-INITIALIZATION.
    OPEN OUTPUT PRINT.
    MOVE 0 TO EOF-FLAG.
    MOVE 57 TO MY-LINE-COUNTER.
    RETURN SORT-FILE AT END MOVE 1 TO EOF-FLAG.
3030-REPORT-BODY.
    IF MY-LINE-COUNTER > 56
        WRITE PRINT-LINE FROM SUBHEADING AFTER PAGE
        MOVE 1 TO MY-LINE-COUNTER.
    MOVE CALL-NUMBER-SR.
    MOVE AUTHOR-SR.
    ADD 2 TO MY-LINE-COUNTER.
    RETURN SORT-FILE AT END MOVE 1 TO EOF-FLAG.
3040-REPORT-TERMINATION.
    CLOSE PRINT.
```

Format a FORTRAN Program

The following program is written in FORTRAN, which is used with mainframe and microcomputers. Its primary applications are in science, mathematics, and engineering.

Learning Activity 5

1. Key the following FORTRAN program. Proof your copy carefully to be sure that every space, punctuation mark, and character is correct. Any error could cause the program to run improperly.
2. Set 1-inch side margins. Begin at the left margin and set a tab seven spaces from the margin.
3. Print a copy and compare it with the model. Mark any uncorrected errors on the printout.

```
C        PROGRAM TO COMPUTE THE VOLUME OF A RIGHT CIRCULAR
CYLINDER
C
C        PROGRAM USES NESTED DO-LOOPS TO INCREMENT DATA
C
         PI=3.141593
         PRINT 5000
  5000   FORMAT ('1')
  50     FORMAT (12X,'HEIGHT',13X,'DIAMETER',13X,'VOLUME')
         DC 100 J=1, 12
         H=FLOAT9J*10)
         PRINT 5C
         PRINT 6C
60       FORMAT (3(10X,10('*'))/)
         DC 110 I-1,15
         D+FLOAT (i*12)
         V+PI**2/4.*H
         PRINT 200,H,D,V
200      FORMAT(3F20.0)
110      CONTINUE
         PRINT1000
1000     FORMAT (//)
100      CONTINUE
         PRINT 5C00
         STOP
         END
```

Format a C Program

The following program is written in C language, which is used primarily with microcomputers. Its primary applications are in science, mathematics, engineering, and business.

Learning Activity 6

1. Key the following C program. Proof your copy carefully to be sure that every space, punctuation mark, and character is correct. Any error could cause the program to run improperly.
2. Set 1-inch side margins. Begin at the left margin and set a tab nine spaces from the margin.
3. Print a copy and compare it with the model. Mark any uncorrected errors on the printout.

```
/* MileKilo */
#include (stdio.h)
void MilesToKilometers(void)
{
          float Miles;
          printf("Miles to Kilometers Conversion\n\n");
          printf("Enter miles to convert: ");
          scanf("%f", &Miles);
          printf("Kilometers: %5.2f\n, Miles * 1.6093);
}
void KilometersToMiles(void)
{
          float Kilometers;
          printf("Kilometers to Miles Conversion\n\n");
          printf("Enter kilometers to convert: ");
          scanf("%f", &Kilometers);
          printf("Miles: %5.2f\n", Kilometers / 1.6093;
}
main()
{
          char ch;
          printf("Miles/Kilometers Conversion
Program\n\n");
          printf("(1) Convert Miles to Kilometers\n"n;
          printf("(2) Convert Kilometers to Miles\n");
          printf("Enter option number: ");
          ch = getch();
          printf("%c\n", ch);
          if (ch == '1')
           MilesToKilometers();
          else
           if (ch == '2')
                KilometersToMiles();
           else
                printf("Bad option entered.\n");
```

Appendix C
Supplemental Drills

These drills can be used for extra practice. The drills labeled Lessons 1-11 should be practiced only after the appropriate lesson has been completed. The drills following Lesson 11 contain all letters of the alphabet; practice on these drills should be delayed until Lesson 11 has been completed.

Lesson 1

```
ded fad flask ask lad; ask dad jak flak as; falls;
salsa lass lad asks fall; add sad dads dak; as alf
a sad lad falls as a fad adds a flask salad; asks;
a sass sad dad adds lads asks; ad jaks add salads;
alas; a lad adds salsa; fad flasks fall salads add
```

Lesson 2

```
tends; attends; lends leases dent lent as kent end
a fad flask attends; jade ants lend sands; last as
dent a tent; lent a jade; jade lends and adds fads
lakes dealt attends leaf deaf fan ale sale need as
ease kent sand end ants; ten tees tested ten leafs
```

Lesson 3

```
The hit health ahead hate shall shell slant leash;
The kid said knit instead; The lite kite aided Ede
Ted and Dad hit it; Tad had said hi; Elsie failed;
Al added Teds jade and said hi; The knife fell at;
Tell Ella and Ted and Tad and Fae and Ded and Elsi
```

Lesson 4

```
The net losses told the tale to all those near Ed;
Rafe, Teri, Ted, and Sissie joined Elsi and Father
Take an order for ten trees and tents, Terrie Fae;
The old elf stole, so did the old kites, tie knot;
A flat train did it, too; She hit the fastest fans
```

Lesson 5

1 Cel felt that she cared; Joe said he did not deal.
2 Rest safe; no one called Ta and Rickie, I said no.
3 Le said that the docks are closed, no one listens.
4 CARLOS and JANE closed the closet doors hard, Rae.
5 Les O. said that the credit classes were canceled.

Lesson 7

1 Marcie: I do need to see the cats, fish, and rat.
2 Boats are safe. Mine is not. A car is safe. Hi.
3 NASA leases land to: Karl, Jane, Mark, and Marci.
4 Ask Mat and Chris to assist. The tent sales fell.
5 The trashes ashes landed on docks B, and M, and D.

Lesson 8

1 Mr. and Mrs. Wallace told the tale about two fish.
2 William wants the rainfall to be in the mountains.
3 I must tell the truth to the auditor of be jailed.
4 Chocolate pies are the best; lemon pies are third.
5 The three purple clocks were placed on the mantel.

Lesson 9

1 Go to the Xerox machine and make ten copies of it.
2 You can do anything, if you think you can and try.
3 Xanaxe is a medicine and is prescribed by doctors.
4 Women had been working for many years. Good work.
5 Six sassy sailors raised taxes on the large ships.

Lesson 10

1 The phone number was two zero two one two one two.
2 Can you go to the Zodiac Club with me tomorrow Jo?
3 Was it advisable to pick up the available waivers?
4 Can you go to or come from the stores immediately?
5 Will you be stopping by the party at a frat house?

Lesson 11

1 The well-known quacks told some very stupid jokes.
2 Once upon a time a quiet lamb lived on a big farm.
3 The up-to-date story was told with a quick finale.
4 The accounting teacher lives in the near East End.
5 Philosophically, I do not know how to answer them.

Two-Letter Word Drills

1 he in on so or of it at if be by ti do ha la it or
2 if it is or no an si in as at no up me en an of on
3 of at or in an it if is to te ti do id di my fa go
4 an is he at me go bo as of it an am co to if at it
5 to no on in or so up fa go am em be ex by me my do

Three-Letter Word Drills

1 how cut big put hot ten lie was per its eve cab
2 too for bag him did gas get out fly old bug cat
3 say day aim big way hat dim sit sin bet did war
4 won all bar eat did cat ton saw tar vat was zip
5 art but cat did eat far gut had ill fog sap tow

Four-Letter Word Drills

1 half mail gear roll must site mark plea good line
2 cold here went open pain toll past tore site dues
3 must want true area quit rely room move dove love
4 sale must take here list hall want mark head take
5 lain cook boys mind pear faze tear vote fade have

Specific Key Drills

A An ad announcing the annual assembly was advertised in American public announcements section.

B Business buys goods and brings better bounty to citizens.

C Careless cars careening across the concrete could cause accidents.

D Did the demise of Dameron Doolittle dampen the party?

E Every easy entry eventually costs in the end.

F Foundations find funds frequently. Funding fads is false and foolish.

G "Good gracious," greeted Gary. Get the garbage off the grate.

H Hassle the harried housewife. How many husbands has she had?

I I will find it. Will it be filled? The dill will fill the pickle with a thrill.

J Justice just joins the jobs. Junior Jackson just jeers jauntily.

K To know how to knot the kite tail without kinks is essential.

M The military wants mastery of the marine and other main markets.

A machine can match the main and major manners of mischief makers.

N The nurse nurtured the neck nerves with new techniques.

O The original ornate object offended the officials.

P Pamela paid the prize for pleasing purple.

Q The quaint queens quickly quoted Quo Vadis and Quintus.

R Ronald roasted the round roll of rare rabbit.

S The sacred scroll was a scientific spoof about some super species.

T The total trip turned to tolerance of tight scheduled trivia.

U It was urgent until the usage of the unit made it unable to unload.

V The value of a good valve became evident as the vapor rose from the vat.

W What woman would wish to work in worse conditions?

X The group text exploited and became excited when they were excluded from the expansion.

Y The yearly trip to see the yoga was nearly canceled.

Z The zebra was one of the dozen shipped to the zoo.

Paragraphs—All Letters

❶ Computers, like any piece of equipment, will need some maintenance. If you do not have the computer checked on a regular basis, then it will surely break down. When the computer is down, the work flow will not be up to par. So good maintenance plans do pay!

❷ In the near future, many more business transactions will be done via computer. When computers are linked with home systems, many people will work at home. This will change many lifestyles and reduce traffic problems. Many new cottage jobs will emerge.

❸ Every clerk needs to know how to set up a set of files. The files need to be arranged in an order that anyone can understand. A filing system that only the person who created it can use is not a good system. Many types of files can be categorized in logical sections. These sections need to relate to the type of business that is conducted.